S0-BUB-634

INSTANT FURNITURE

INSTANT FURNITURE

Low-cost, well-designed, easy-to-assemble tables, chairs, couches, beds, desks, and storage systems

PETER S. STAMBERG

with designs by Gerrit J. Rietveld, Carlo Scarpa, Kazuhide Takahama, Enzo Mari, Ira Saltz, and Peter S. Stamberg

Photography by the Globus Brothers

VNR VAN NOSTRAND REINHOLD COMPANY

NEW YORK CINCINNATI TORONTO LONDON MELBOURNE

Dedicated to Dino Gavina

Copyright © 1976 by Litton Educational Publishing, Inc.
Library of Congress Catalog Card Number 75-40933
ISBN 0-442-27935-3 (cloth)
ISBN 0-442-27934-5 (paper)

All rights reserved. No part of this work covered by the
copyright hereon may be reproduced or used in any form or
by any means—graphic, electronic, or mechanical, including
photocopying, recording, taping, or information storage and
retrieval systems—without written permission of the publisher.
Printed in the United States of America

Designed by Loudan Enterprises

Published in 1976 by Van Nostrand Reinhold Company
A Division of Litton Educational Publishing, Inc.
450 West 33rd Street
New York, NY 10001

Van Nostrand Reinhold Limited
1410 Birchmount Road
Scarborough, Ontario M1P 2E7, Canada

Van Nostrand Reinhold Australia Pty. Ltd.
17 Queen Street
Mitcham, Victoria 3132, Australia

Van Nostrand Reinhold Company Ltd.
Molly Millars Lane
Wokingham, Berkshire, England

16 15 14 13 12 11 10 9 8 7 6 5 4 3

Library of Congress Cataloging in Publication Data

Stamberg, Peter S
  Instant furniture.

  Includes index.
  1. Furniture making. I. Title.
TT195.S7   684.1'04   75-40933
ISBN 0-442-27935-3
ISBN 0-442-27934-5 pbk.

Designs by Gerrit T. Rietveld manufactured exclusively by Cassina under license from the Rietveld
estate and distributed exclusively in the United
States by Atelier International, Ltd.

Designs by Enzo Mari, Carlo Scarpa, and Kazuhide
Takahama manufactured in Europe exclusively
by Simon International under license from the
designers.

Designs by Enzo Mari, Carlo Scarpa, Peter S. Stamberg, and Kazuhide Takahama manufactured in
the United States exclusively by Stamberg Metafurniture, Inc., under license from Simon International
and the designers.

The design by Ira Saltz reproduced by permission
of the designer, who retains all rights for commercial
manufacturing.

All drawings by Peter S. Stamberg except Sh'Matta
upholstery by Al Jarnow, Jr.

Photography by the Globus Brothers.

CONTENTS

INTRODUCTION

Stamberg Metafurniture is low-technology design for inexpensive do-it-yourself furniture that anyone can build from precut wood, glue, and finishing nails.

The hand is quicker than the eye—how to choose your first piece of metafurniture. If you have never worked with wood before, the first piece you build is extremely important: the simpler, the better. Be careful—designs that look simple in the drawings and photographs can be very tricky. The designs that the beginning builder will have the least difficulty with are those with the fewest number of stars (denoting variable dimensions) in the materials list. For example, the JSJ chair (design 21) and the Rabbit chair (design 10) have no stars in the materials list. The ICS table (design 2) and the EFFE table (design 3) have relatively few stars. By contrast, in the Vocastra couches every linear dimension has a star.

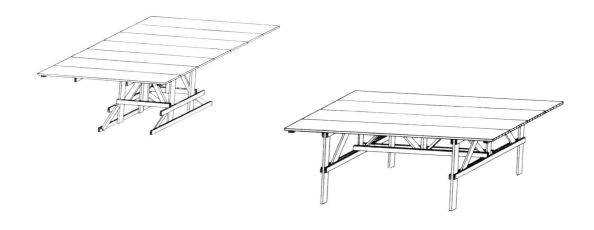

How to build your first piece of metafurniture. Once you have selected your first piece of metafurniture, refer to the key design for the construction method. The designs are arranged according to construction type: 1 through 13 are truss designs; 14 through 34, slab designs. (Designs 22 and 25 have slight individual eccentricities, so for the sake of clarity they are also explained in detail.) If you have chosen a truss design, refer to design 1 for construction details. If you have selected a slab design, refer to design 14. For all tabletops refer to design 14. The step-by-step instructions for the key design will familiarize you with the techniques for that particular type. Once you begin to understand the construction, you can start to improvise.

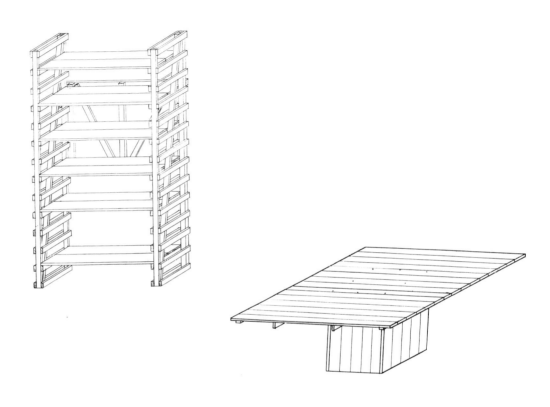

When you are ready to order wood, shop around. Lumber prices constantly fluctuate. But don't despair—although the price of wood is rising, it is still less expensive than metal, glass, stone, or plastic. The supply of wood is not limitless, but it does replenish itself fairly rapidly—more so than metal or stone at any rate! Wood is light in weight and very flexible. And, finally, the assembly time of most of the furniture designs in this book is probably less than what you would spend shopping for a less functional, less individual, and more expensive piece of furniture from a store or manufacturer. All the designs in the book are built of #2 common pine. (The number refers to the quality, or grade, of the wood: #1 is clear pine, containing no knots; #3 has more knots, warps, and cups and is not as well cut; #2 is an in-between grade.) The starting carpenter will fare well with pine because of its wide availability, resistance to splitting and warping, and ease in cutting. If you don't want knots in your wood, order #1 clear pine. Clear pine costs considerably more than common pine, but if knots do not fit into your future, clear pine will eliminate the problem.

At the beginning of each design you will find a materials list. This list tells you the section (size) of each piece to order, the length of each piece, the quantity of each length, and the positions in which you will use each piece. When you order the wood from the list, you must keep in mind the fact that the section appears in what is called *nominal size*. Wood is ordered by nominal size, but what you get is not exactly that size. For example, if you ask for a 1″ × 2″ (one-by-two) piece of wood, you will probably get a piece approximately ¾″ × 1¾″; if you ask for a piece of wood 1″ × 8″ (one-by-eight), you will get a piece approximately ¾″ × 7½″. These are called the *actual sizes*. The reason for this discrepancy is as follows: when a log enters a lumber mill, it is cut into various-sized pieces—1″ × 2″, for example. The wood is then dried in a kiln, however, which causes some shrinkage, and after drying it is trimmed again to smooth the surfaces. Here is a comparative list of what measurements you can expect, but actual sizes may vary to some extent from mill to mill.

Nominal Size	Actual Size
1″ × 2″	¾″ × 1¾″
1″ × 3″	¾″ × 2½″
1″ × 4″	¾″ × 3½″
1″ × 6″	¾″ × 5½″
1″ × 8″	¾″ × 7½″
1″ × 10″	¾″ × 9¼″
1″ × 12″	¾″ × 11¼″

Whenever you see a star (*) next to a dimension in this book, beware. The star means that the dimension may vary depending on the actual "actual size" of the pieces that cross the starred dimension. This problem arises when several pieces butt against one another and a crosspiece ties them together.

For example, in the tabletop in design 14, fifteen one-by-fours butt together, and four one-by-twos hold them in place. Depending on the actual "actual size" of the one-by-fours, the one-by-twos may vary in length. The dimensions listed are derived from the perfect dimensions of a one-by-four as ¾″ × 3½″. To find the actual length of the one-by-twos, place the fifteen one-by-fours together and measure them. If you cut the lengths yourself, you will have no problem at all. If you have the lengths precut at a lumberyard, explain the situation to the person cutting the wood. He can cut the top pieces first, then you can place them together to measure and finally cut the true length of the one-by-twos. The ¾″ dimension of a 1″ × (pronounced "one by") is relatively constant from mill to mill and should pose no problem.

Construction of the designs requires only one nail size, a 1¼" wire brad. You can purchase these nails at most hardware stores and lumberyards. Wire brads come in various gauges (thicknesses). A #16 gauge is the most common, but slight variations will work just as well. Only one glue is required: use any white glue such as Elmer's.

Finishing materials required are paint, varnish, and stain. In painting raw wood, you should always apply an undercoat of paint before painting the final color. With the undercoat high-gloss colors will give you a long-lasting, attractive finish. Stains and varnishes require extremely careful application, since they accentuate imperfections rather than hiding them. Before applying stains or varnishes, carefully sand all surfaces and edges to remove rough spots, splinters, marks, and stains. Then repeat with fine sandpaper to obtain the smoothest possible surface. To stain wood, first apply a base coat of stain, then apply the stain, and last apply a coat of varnish or polyurethane to protect the stain. Since the exact method varies with the product, for best results consult the manufacturer's instructions printed on the can. If you choose a clear varnish, three coats will give you a very strong, long-lasting finish. Between each coat you should smooth the surfaces with very fine sandpaper or steel wool. Before doing so, however, consult the manufacturer's instructions for best results.

Final assembly of a piece will pose no problems if you keep one thing in mind: isolate the elements! For example, while the ICS table (design 2) may look quite complex on the surface, if you isolate the elements, you will find it extremely easy to build. The table consists of five elements: four trusses and the tabletop. First construct two identical trusses using one B piece, three C pieces, two E pieces, two F pieces, and two G pieces for each. Next construct two identical trusses using two D pieces and three F pieces for each. Then assemble the four trusses into the base. Finally construct the tabletop using seven A pieces and two B pieces. Attach the top to the base and you will have a table.

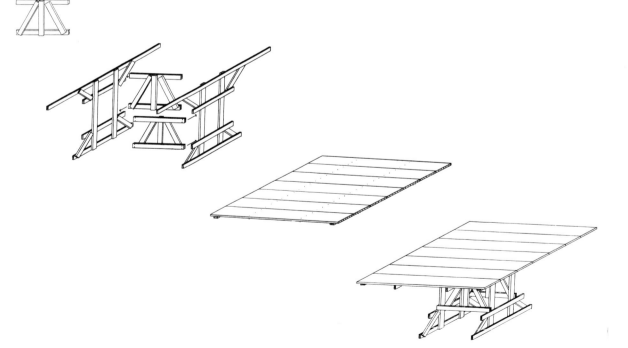

In fastening two pieces together, you should always apply glue to the joint before nailing. If you follow this simple procedure, you will have no difficulty.

1. Use a solid, steady work surface. If you try to nail on a springy table or a rug, the wood will bounce, making it very difficult to drive the nails.
2. Lay out the pieces for the element in exact position.
3. With a pencil lightly mark the position of the upper pieces on the lower pieces.
4. With a pencil mark the positions of all nails.
5. Remove the upper pieces, marked for nailing, from the lower pieces, marked for positioning.
6. Start nails into all the spots you have marked. Drive the nails far enough so that the points just barely penetrate the other side of the wood. A hammer is easier to manipulate if you hold it near the end of the handle rather than towards the head.
7. Apply glue to the lower pieces between the marks inscribed according to step (3) of this procedure.
8. Carefully replace the upper pieces, with their started nails, on the lower pieces.
9. Drive in the nails. Before driving each nail make certain that the piece has not bounced out of position from hammering previous nails.

If you try to apply glue before starting the nails, you will find that when you begin to drive the nails, the pieces will slide around quite a bit on the slick surface of the wet glue. By starting the nails in advance and letting them protrude slightly through the pieces, you can tack the pieces together just by placing them in position. Whenever possible you should allow the glue on the completed components to dry before assembling the finished piece.

The drawing style used in this book is referred to by several names: axonometric, oblique isometric, or paraline projection. The main advantage of this style is that every dimension remains true rather than diminishing, as in perspective. This makes the drawings fairly easy to read. However, this style does create great visual distortion. Therefore, do not try to judge the final appearance of a design by the drawings but by the photographs.

All the dimensions required to build the pieces are included in the drawings (successive pieces have the same section measurements as the preceding pieces unless denoted otherwise). If you have trouble finding a dimension that you think should be included, remember that (1) the length and width of a member can be found by referring to the materials list at the beginning of each set of drawings; and (2) the thickness of all members is ¾". In several drawings in which many dimensions are given, the ¾" dimension has often been eliminated for reasons of visual simplification. Therefore, when you see a drawing with small dimension marks and no number, remember that the space is ¾".

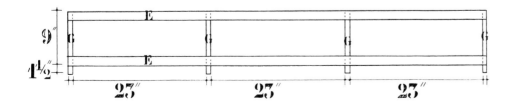

DESIGN 1

Scala   Designer: Enzo Mari

Piece	Section	Quantity	Length	Use
A	1″ × 2″	2	80″	side truss diagonals
B		4	79″	side truss verticals
C		2	43″	rear truss horizontals
D		2	39″	rear truss diagonals
E		3	36″	rear truss verticals
F		56	11¾″	side truss horizontals
G	1″ × 6″	10	*39¾″	shelves

1

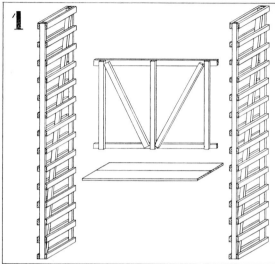

1. This shelving unit is composed of two types of trusses: *enclosed* and *open*.

2

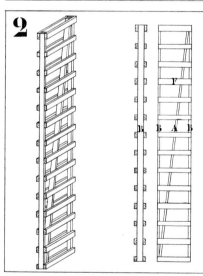

2. The first basic units to build are the support trusses. They are enclosed trusses.

3

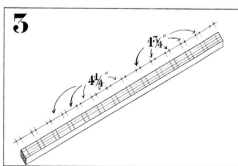

3. Place the four B pieces on edge side by side. With a pencil and a T-square inscribe lines across them in 7¾" and 4¼" increments as shown. Then turn the pieces over and inscribe lines on the opposite edges in the same increments.

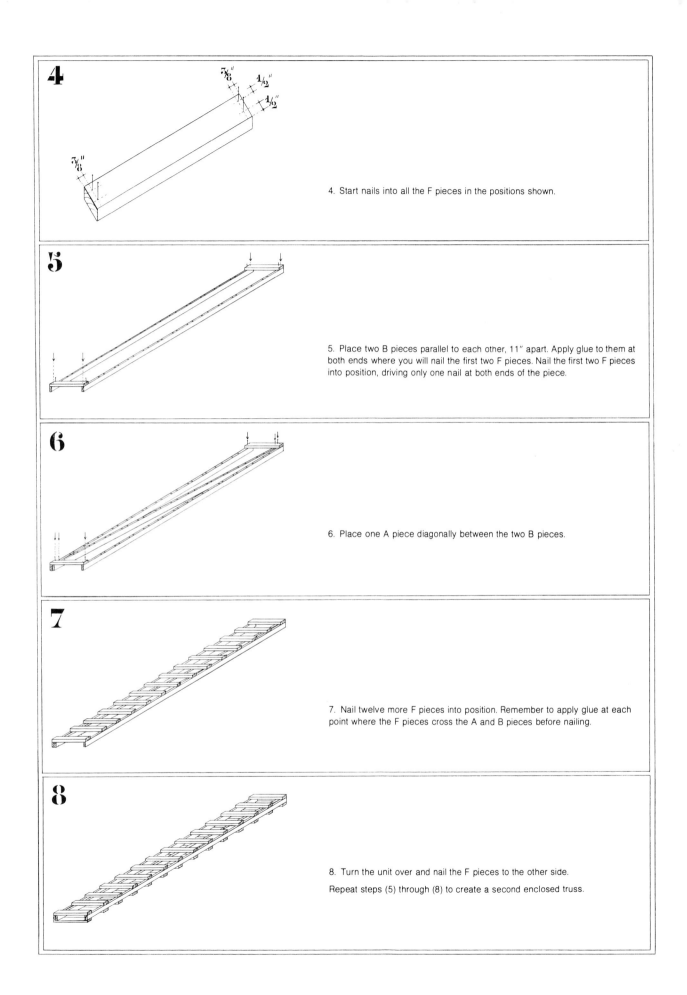

4. Start nails into all the F pieces in the positions shown.

5. Place two B pieces parallel to each other, 11″ apart. Apply glue to them at both ends where you will nail the first two F pieces. Nail the first two F pieces into position, driving only one nail at both ends of the piece.

6. Place one A piece diagonally between the two B pieces.

7. Nail twelve more F pieces into position. Remember to apply glue at each point where the F pieces cross the A and B pieces before nailing.

8. Turn the unit over and nail the F pieces to the other side.

Repeat steps (5) through (8) to create a second enclosed truss.

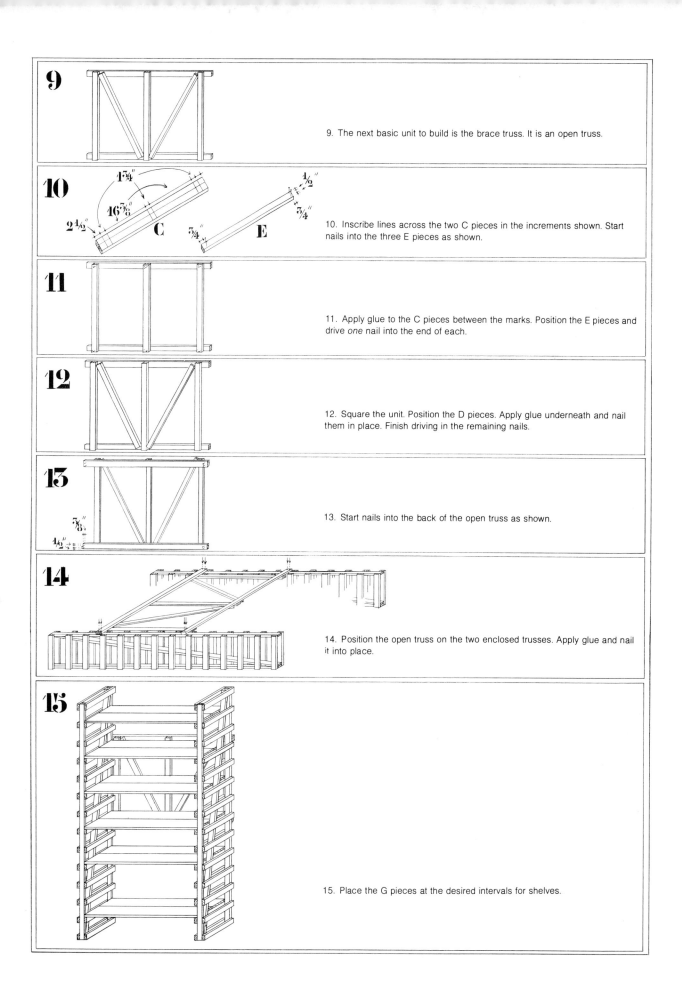

9 9. The next basic unit to build is the brace truss. It is an open truss.

10 10. Inscribe lines across the two C pieces in the increments shown. Start nails into the three E pieces as shown.

11 11. Apply glue to the C pieces between the marks. Position the E pieces and drive *one* nail into the end of each.

12 12. Square the unit. Position the D pieces. Apply glue underneath and nail them in place. Finish driving in the remaining nails.

13 13. Start nails into the back of the open truss as shown.

14 14. Position the open truss on the two enclosed trusses. Apply glue and nail it into place.

15 15. Place the G pieces at the desired intervals for shelves.

DESIGN 2

ICS   Designer: Enzo Mari

Piece	Section	Quantity	Length	Use
A	1″ × 8″	7	52½″	top
B	1″ × 2″	4	*52½″	top braces
C		6	27¼″	large truss verticals and lower horizontals
D		4	21¾″	small truss horizontals
E		4	19½″	large truss middle horizontals
F		10	12″	small truss verticals & horizontals; large truss top diagonals
G		4	9″	large truss bottom diagonals

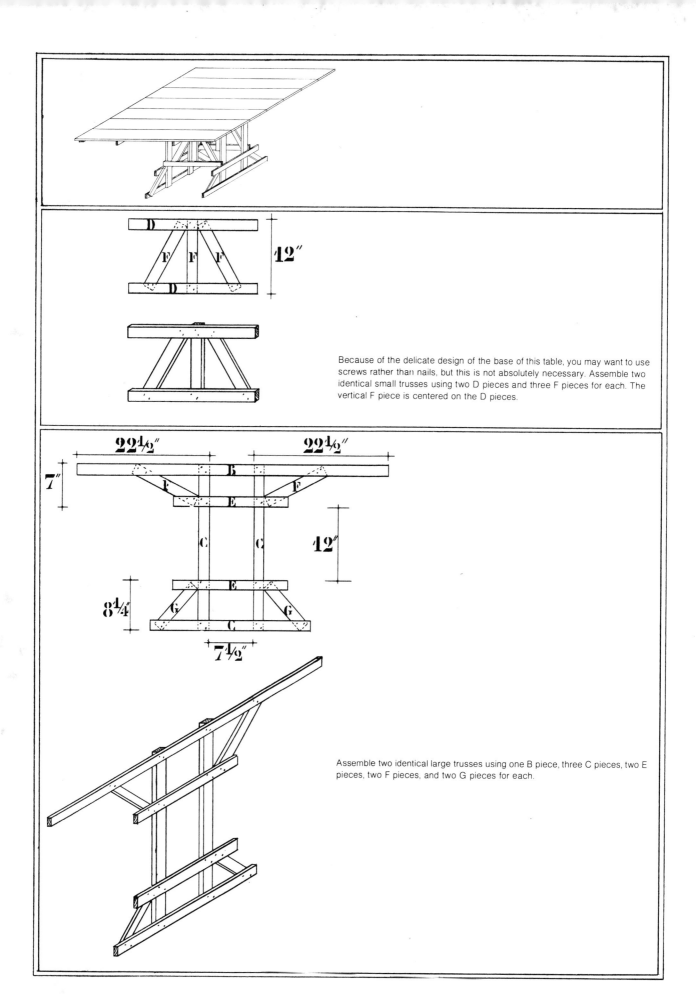

12"

Because of the delicate design of the base of this table, you may want to use screws rather than nails, but this is not absolutely necessary. Assemble two identical small trusses using two D pieces and three F pieces for each. The vertical F piece is centered on the D pieces.

22½"   22½"

7"

12"

8¼

7½"

Assemble two identical large trusses using one B piece, three C pieces, two E pieces, two F pieces, and two G pieces for each.

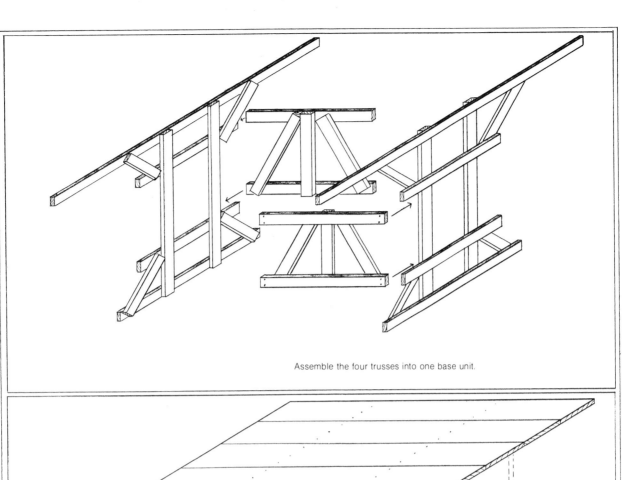

Assemble the four trusses into one base unit.

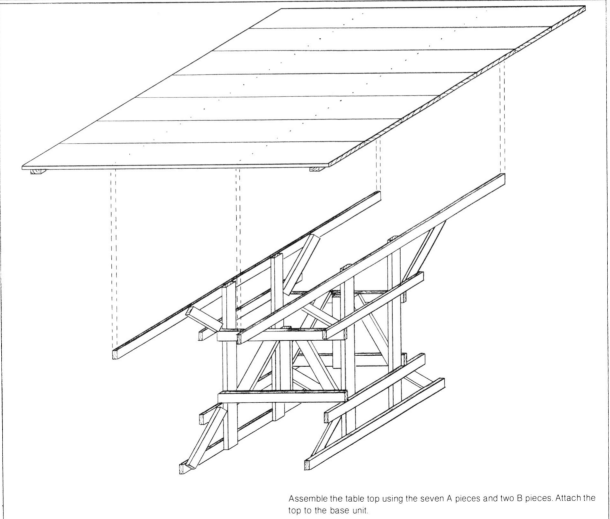

Assemble the table top using the seven A pieces and two B pieces. Attach the
top to the base unit.

DESIGN 3

EFFE   Designer: Enzo Mari

Piece	Section	Quantity	Length	Use
A	1″ × 8″	4	79″	top
B	1″ × 2″	4	51″	long truss horizontals
C		10	*30″	side truss horizontals & top braces
D		4	27¼″	legs
E		4	16½″	side truss diagonals
F		4	14″	long truss diagonals
G		2	14¾″	long truss verticals
H		3	10½″	long truss verticals

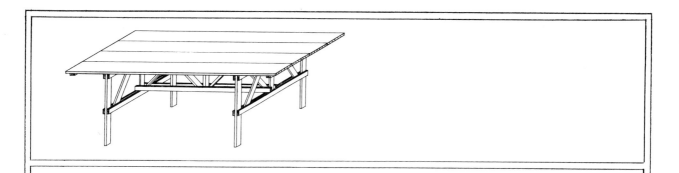

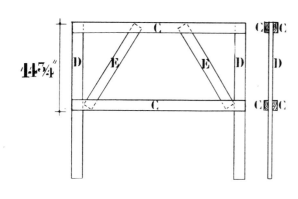

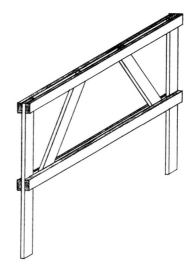

First construct two identical end trusses using four C pieces, two D pieces, and two E pieces for each.

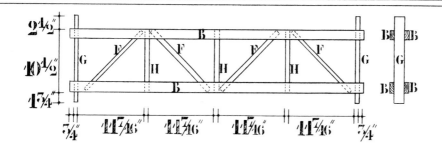

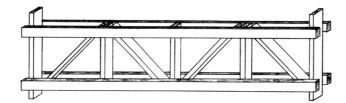

Construct one cross truss using four B pieces, four F pieces, two G pieces, and three H pieces.

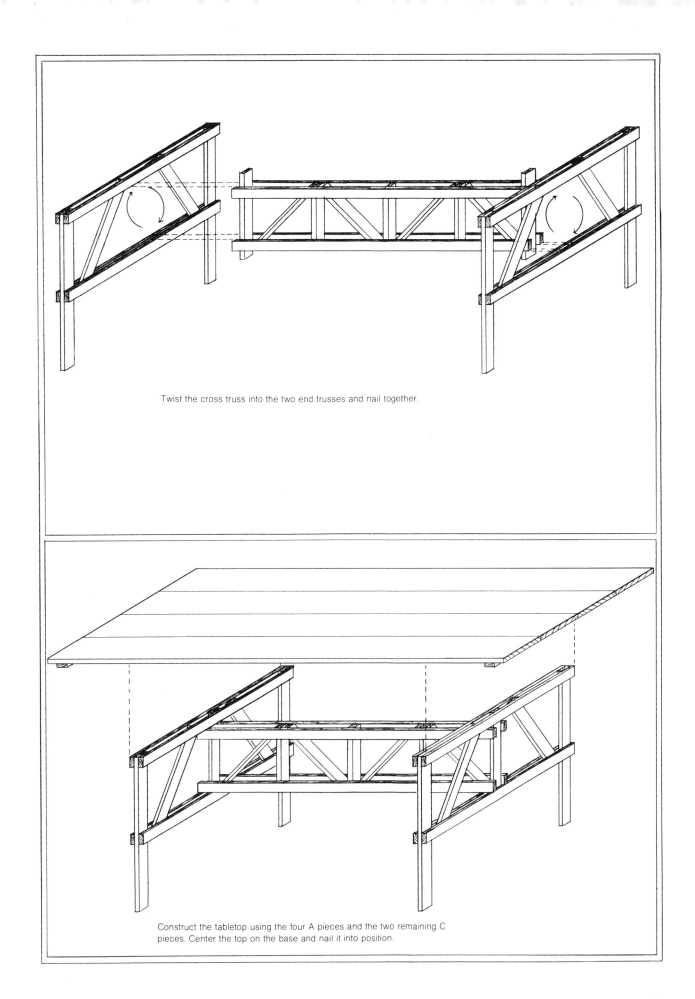

Twist the cross truss into the two end trusses and nail together.

Construct the tabletop using the four A pieces and the two remaining C pieces. Center the top on the base and nail it into position.

DESIGN 4

Daniel 1   Designer: Stamberg

Piece	Section	Quantity	Length	Use
A	1″ × 2″	24	27″	side truss horizontals
B		4	25″	side truss diagonals
C		6	24″	side truss verticals
D		6	27″	back truss outside horizontals
E		6	24″	back truss inside horizontals
F		2	25½″	back truss diagonals
C		5	24″	back truss verticals
C		4	24″	front truss horizontals
G		2	10½″	front truss verticals
C		9	24″	seat

For upholstery see page 34.

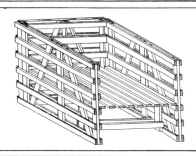

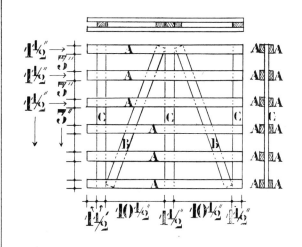

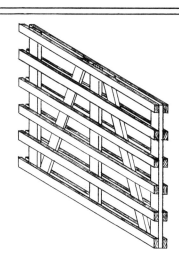

Construct two identical side trusses using twelve A pieces, two B pieces, and three C pieces for each. Since the exact "actual size" of the 1"-×-2" members may be larger than indicated, the 3" dimension may be smaller accordingly.

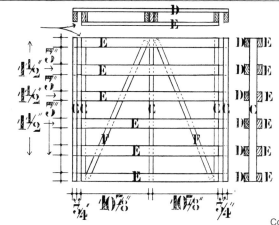

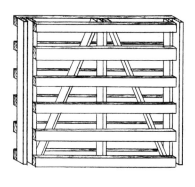

Construct the back truss using five C pieces, six D pieces, six E pieces, and two F pieces. Make sure the space between the two C pieces is ¾" at both ends so that the side trusses fit easily into the slots.

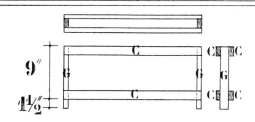

Construct the front truss using four C pieces and two G pieces.

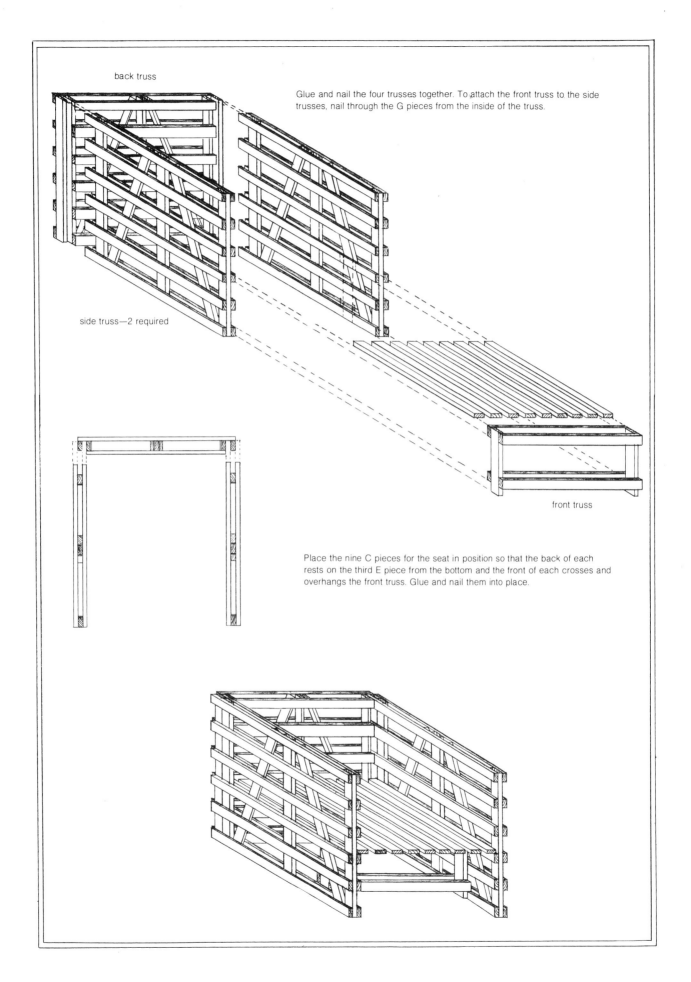

back truss

Glue and nail the four trusses together. To attach the front truss to the side trusses, nail through the G pieces from the inside of the truss.

side truss—2 required

front truss

Place the nine C pieces for the seat in position so that the back of each rests on the third E piece from the bottom and the front of each crosses and overhangs the front truss. Glue and nail them into place.

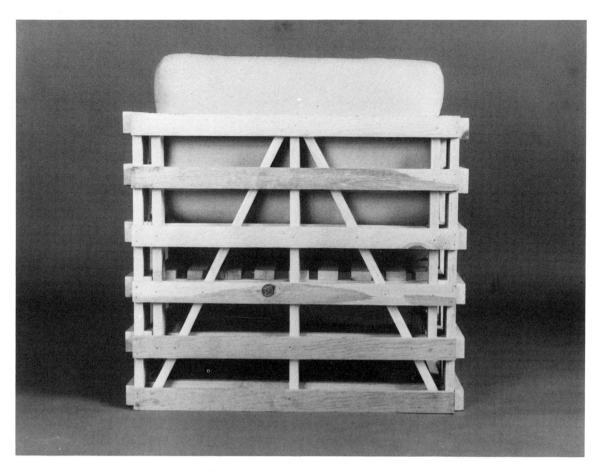

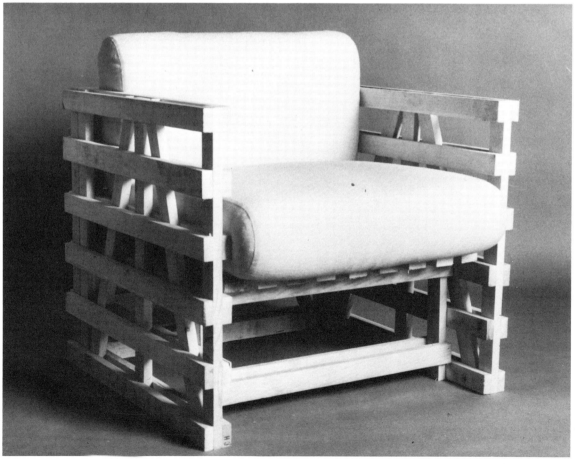

DESIGN 5

Daniel 2   Designer: Stamberg

Piece	Section	Quantity	Length	Use
A	1" × 2"	24	27"	side truss horizontals
B		4	25"	side truss diagonals
C		6	24"	side truss verticals
D		6	51"	back truss outside horizontals
E		6	48"	back truss inside horizontals
F		2	31"	back truss diagonals
C		5	24"	back truss verticals
E		4	48"	front truss horizontals
G		3	10½"	front truss verticals
C		18	24"	seat

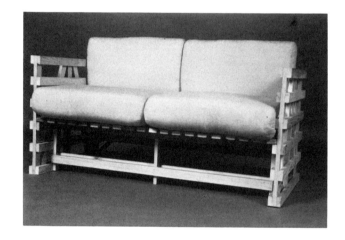

For upholstery see page 34.

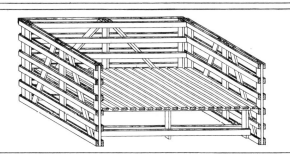

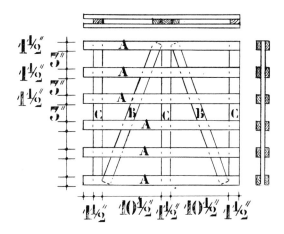

Construct two identical side trusses using twelve A pieces, two B pieces, and three C pieces for each. Since the exact "actual size" of the 1"-×-2" members may vary, the 3" dimension may vary accordingly.

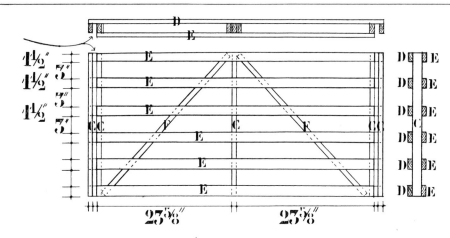

Construct the back truss using six D pieces, six E pieces, two F pieces, and five C pieces. Make sure that the space between the two C pieces is ¾" at either end of the truss so that the side trusses fit easily into the slots.

Construct the front truss using four E pieces and three G pieces.

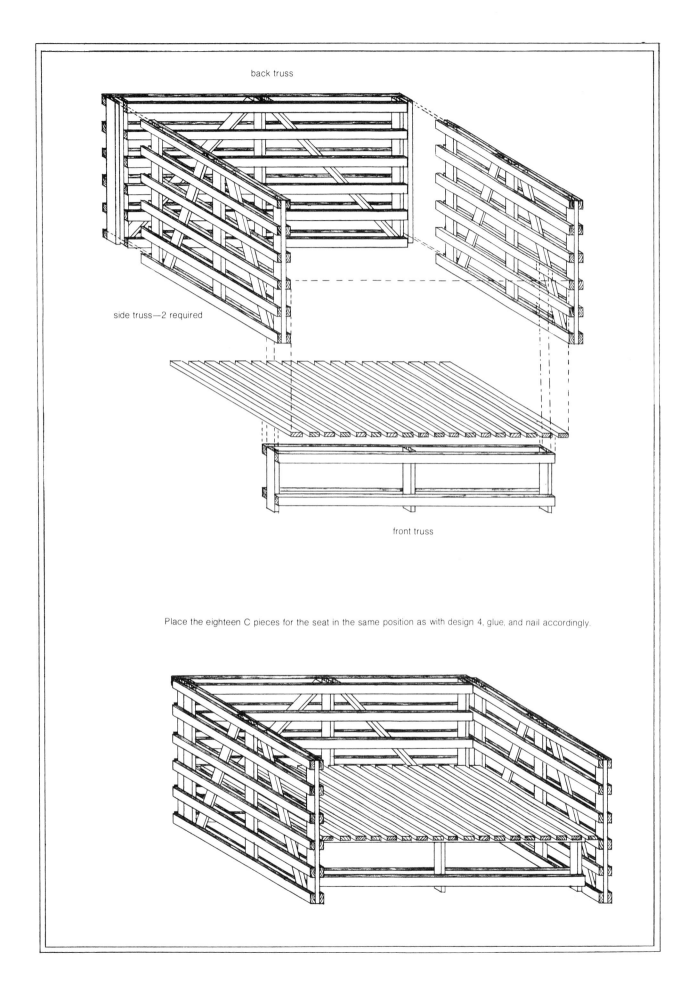

back truss

side truss—2 required

front truss

Place the eighteen C pieces for the seat in the same position as with design 4, glue, and nail accordingly.

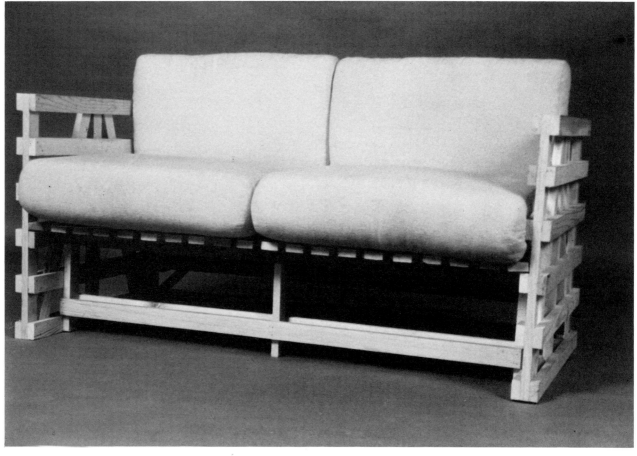

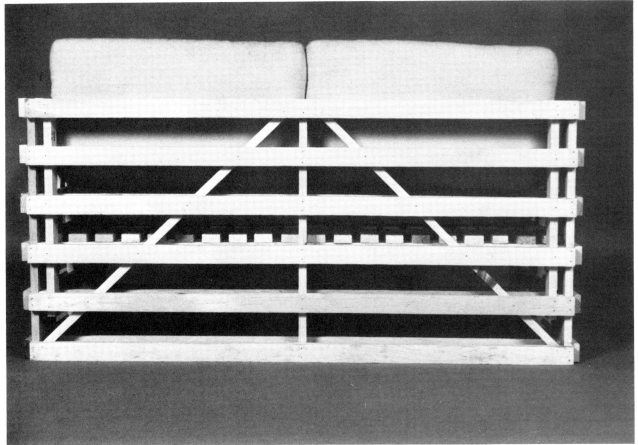

Daniel 3   Designer: Stamberg

Piece	Section	Quantity	Length	Use
A	1″ × 2″	24	27″	side truss horizontals
B		4	25′	side truss diagonals
C		6	24″	side truss verticals
D		6	75″	back truss outside horizontals
E		6	72″	back truss inside horizontals
F		2	41″	back truss diagonals
C		5	24″	back truss verticals
E		4	72″	front truss horizontals
G		4	10½″	front truss verticals
C		27	24″	seat

Construction follows the same plan as for designs 4 and 5.

Because the Daniel armchair and couches have platform bases, the upholstery cushions require two densities of foam as well as a layer of fiberfill. All cushions consist of a block of high-density foam 3″ thick; a block of medium-density foam 3″ thick; and a layer of 2″-thick fiberfill batting placed over the top and wrapped around the front edge.

Daniel 1 requires one seat cushion 24″ wide × 28″ deep and one back cushion 24″ wide × 12″ high. Daniel 2 requires two seat cushions 24″ wide × 28″ deep and two back cushions 24″ wide × 12″ high. Daniel 3 requires three seat cushions 24″ wide × 28″ deep and three back cushions 24″ wide × 12″ high.

Upholstery for the Vocastra series (designs 27 and 28) follows the same model. Cushions will vary in size depending on the actual finished size of the piece. The depth of the cushions, however, will remain a constant 28″ for the seat and 12″ for the back. The width of the cushions will be the same dimension as the length of the C pieces.

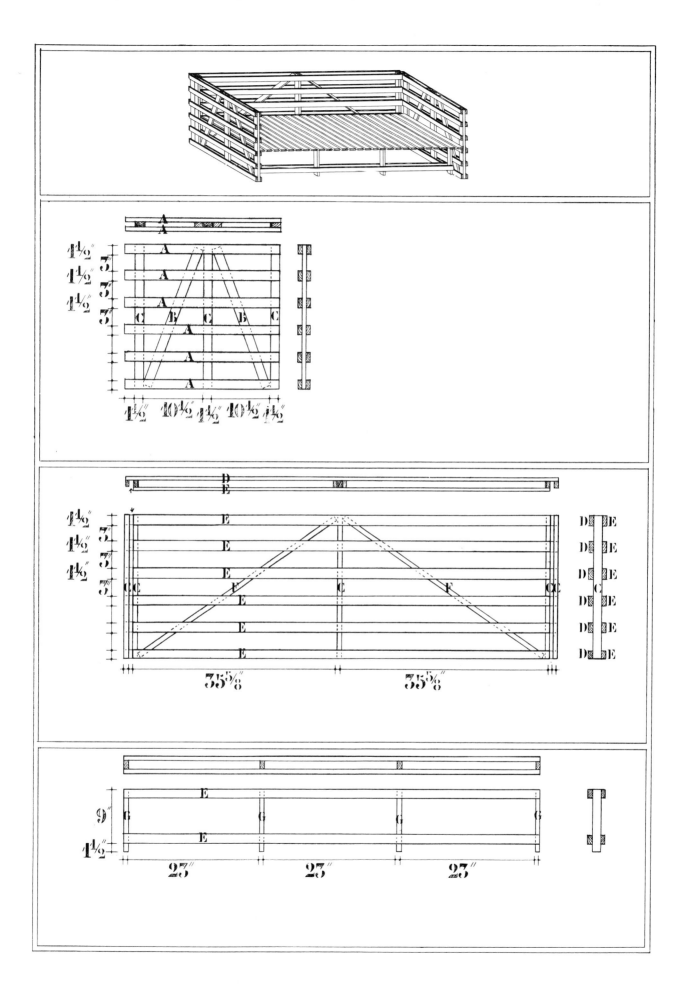

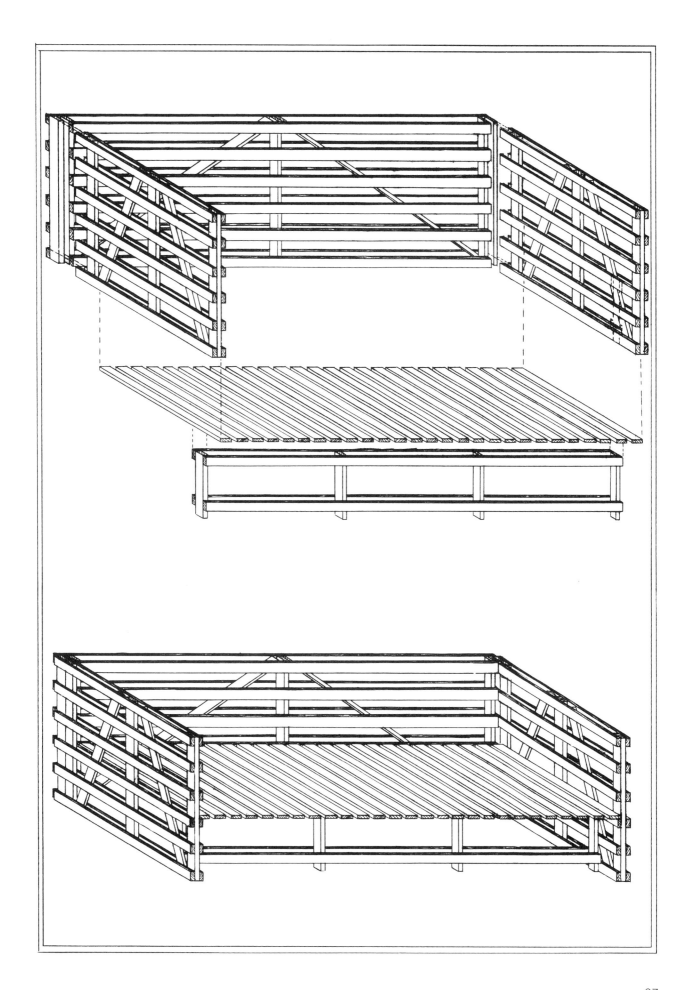

Sh'Matta 1   Designer: Stamberg

Piece	Section	Quantity	Length	Use
A	1″ × 2″	12	27″	side truss horizontals
B		8	22″	side truss verticals & diagonals
C		2	**21½″**	side truss middle verticals
D		7	24″	side truss back verticals, rear truss vertical & diagonals, & seat slats
E		16	30″	rear truss horizontals & front truss horizontals
F		1	10½″	front truss vertical
G		2	14″	front truss diagonals

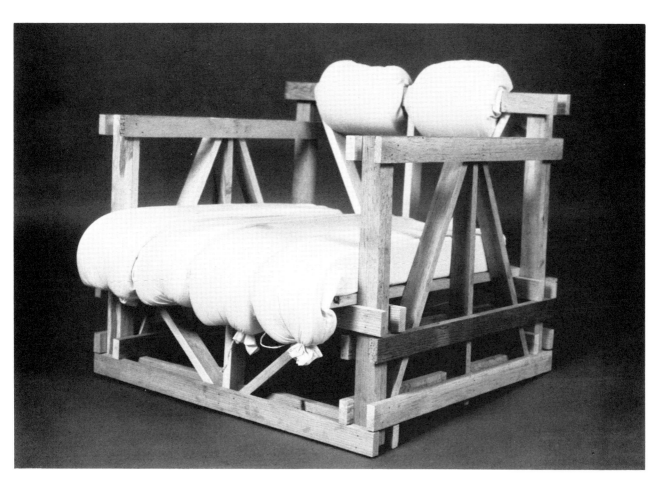

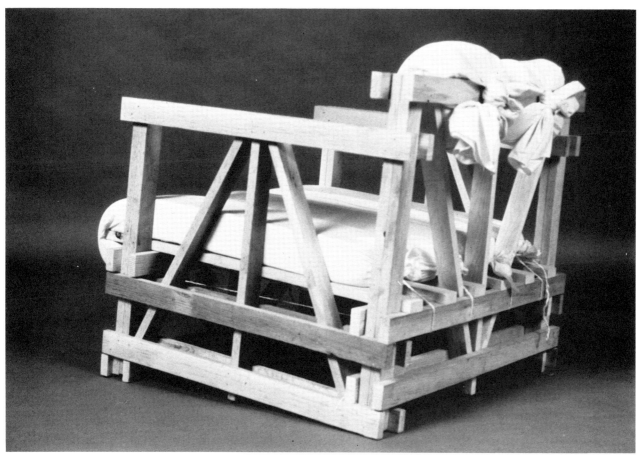

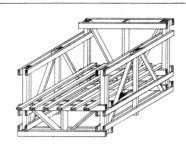

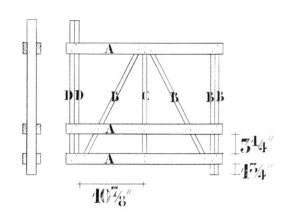

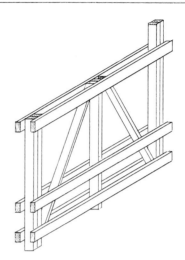

3¼″
1¾″

10⅞″

Construct two identical side trusses using six A pieces, four B pieces, one C piece, and two D pieces for each. The first step of this assembly is to nail together two B pieces and two D pieces for the front and back vertical of each truss.

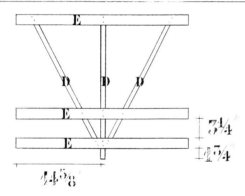

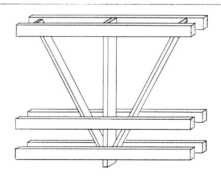

3¼
1¾

4⅝

Construct the rear truss using three D pieces and six E pieces.

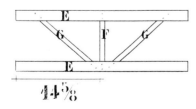

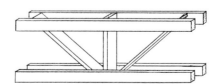

4⅝

Construct the front truss using four E pieces, one F piece, and two G pieces.

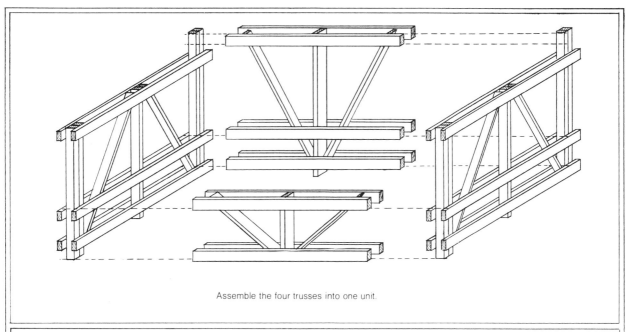

Assemble the four trusses into one unit.

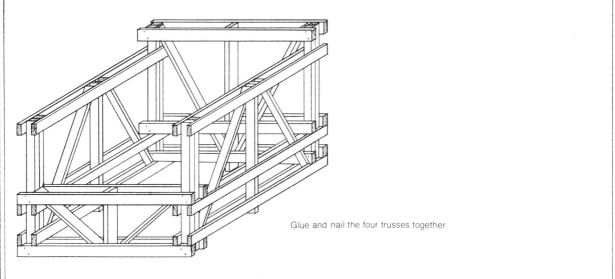

Glue and nail the four trusses together.

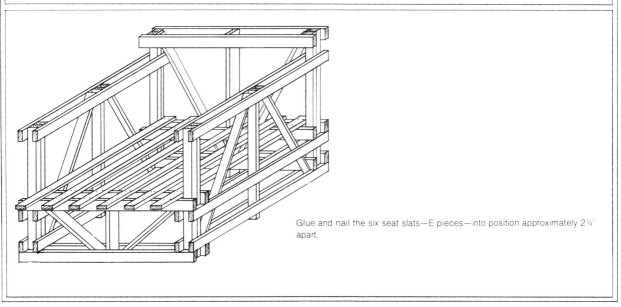

Glue and nail the six seat slats—E pieces—into position approximately 2¾" apart.

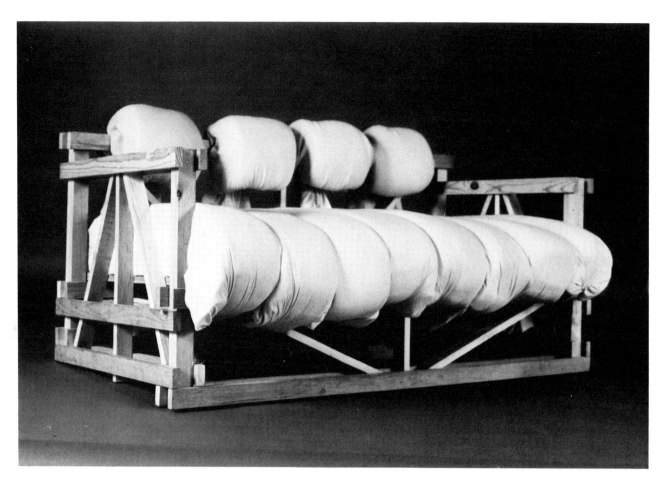

Upholstery for the Sh'Matta series—armchair, love seat, or couch—requires no sewing. It consists of two basic units: the seat cushion and the back cushion. Each of the units requires four elements: (a) fabric, (b) a piece of fiberfill batting, (c) a medium-density foam block, and (d) a high-density foam block.

Choose a sturdy but lightweight fabric such as cotton muslin or canvas. The fabric must be light enough to hold a knot. The fabric for the seat unit should measure at least 27″ by 96″. A few extra inches in each dimension will make the fabric easier to work with, but the final appearance will be slightly less tidy. The fabric for the back unit should measure 36″ by 44″.

Fiberfill batting, available in the upholstery department of most department stores, comes in many thicknesses. The Sh'Matta series requires 2″-thick sheets. If this thickness is not available, a composite of a few layers of thinner material will do just as well. For the seat unit use a piece 6″ × 32″ × 2″ (thick). For the back unit use a piece 8″ × 12″ × 2″ (thick).

The core requires two densities of foam: one for support and the other for softness. Each seat unit requires one block of high-density foam 6″ × 32″ × 3″ (thick) and one block of medium-density foam exactly the same size. Each back unit requires one block of high-density foam 8″ × 12″ × 1½″ (thick) and one block of medium-density foam 8″ × 12″ × 3″ (thick).

Quantities: each Sh'Matta 1 requires four seat units and two back units; each Sh'Matta 2 requires eight seat units and four back units; each Sh'Matta 3 requires twelve seat units and six back units.

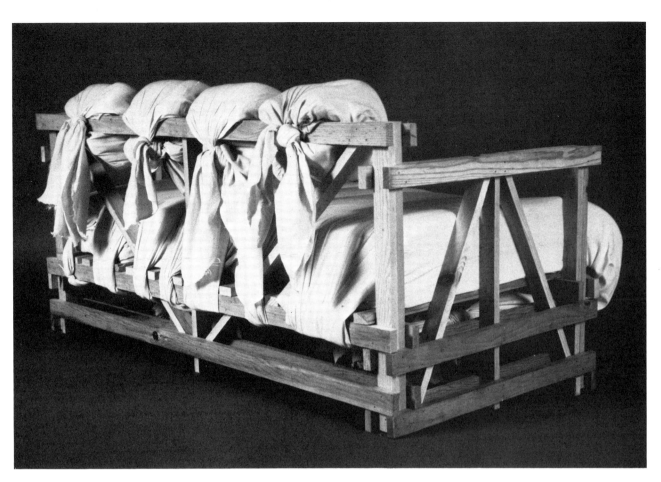

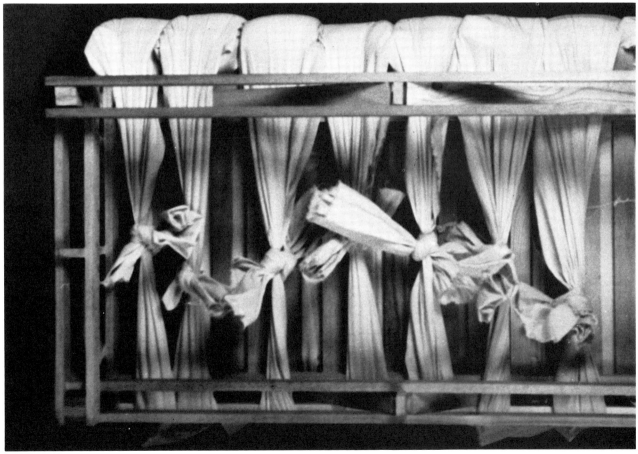

Procedure for the seat unit is described below.

1. Place the fabric on a large work surface. Place the fiberfill on top of the fabric in the center, the medium-density foam on the fiberfill, and the high-density foam on top.

2. Fold the long edges of the fabric around the foam and fiberfill blocks.

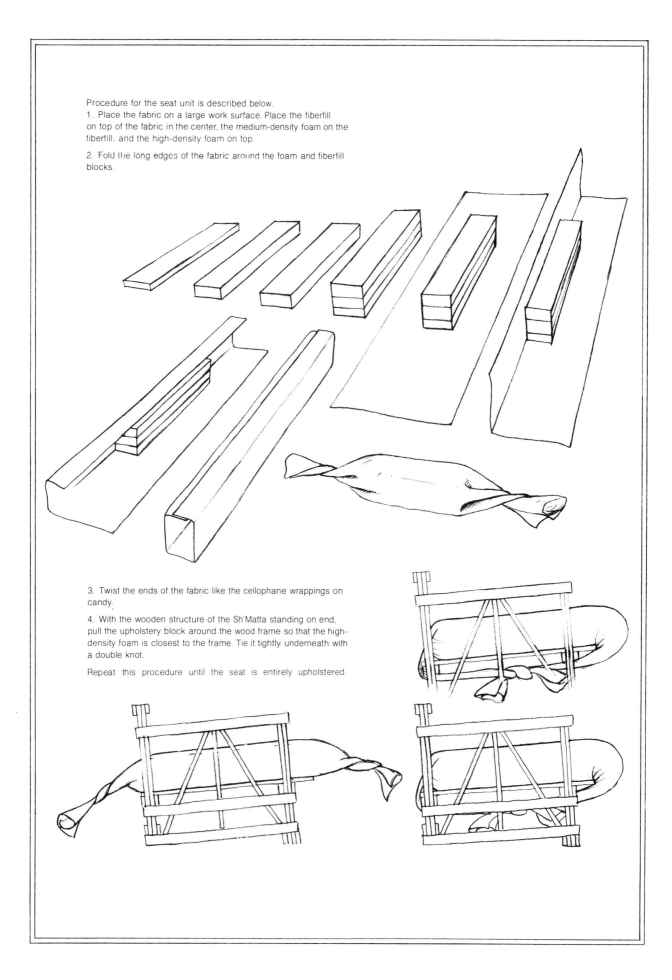

3. Twist the ends of the fabric like the cellophane wrappings on candy.

4. With the wooden structure of the Sh'Matta standing on end, pull the upholstery block around the wood frame so that the high-density foam is closest to the frame. Tie it tightly underneath with a double knot.

Repeat this procedure until the seat is entirely upholstered.

Procedure for the back unit is explained below.

1. Place the fabric on a large work surface. Diagonally center the fiberfill on the fabric. Place the medium-density foam on the fiberfill, then the high-density foam on top.

2. Fold two opposite corners around the foam and fiberfill block, leaving the remaining tails as long as possible.

3. Twist the fabric tails like cellophane wrapping.

4. Pull the upholstery block around the horizontal members of the back of the Sh'Matta frame, again with the high-density foam closest to the frame. Tie it tightly with a double knot.

Repeat this procedure until you have covered the back with the required number of upholstery blocks.

(The upholstery for the Sh'Matta 1 chair shown in the photographs was an experimental prototype. Please refer to the photographs of the Sh'Matta 2 love seat for the final appearance.)

Sh'Matta 2   Designer: Stamberg

Piece	Section	Quantity	Length	Use
A	1″ × 2″	12	27″	side truss horizontals
B		8	22″	side truss front verticals & diagonals
C		2	21½″	side truss middle verticals
D		7	24″	side truss rear verticals, rear truss verticals, & front truss diagonals
E		10	53¼″	rear & front truss horizontals
F		2	31″	rear truss diagonals
G		1	10½″	front truss vertical
H		18	30″	seat slats

For upholstery see pages 42 to 45.

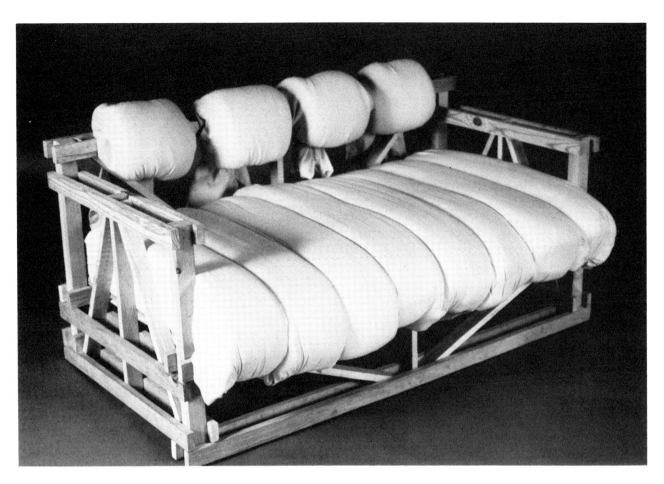

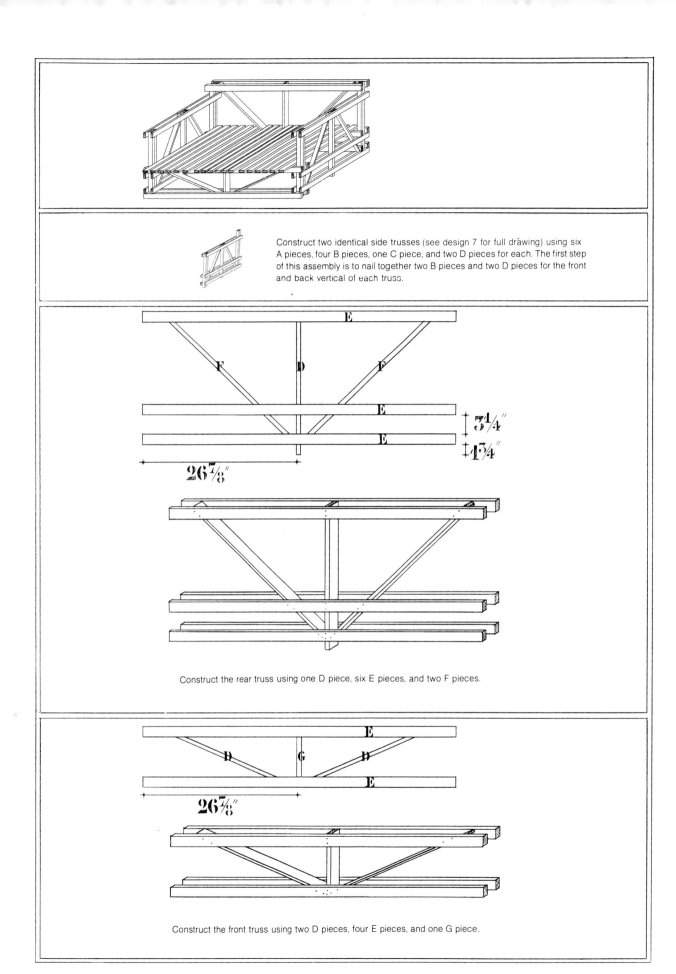

Construct two identical side trusses (see design 7 for full drawing) using six A pieces, four B pieces, one C piece, and two D pieces for each. The first step of this assembly is to nail together two B pieces and two D pieces for the front and back vertical of each truss.

26⅞″

3¼″

1¾″

Construct the rear truss using one D piece, six E pieces, and two F pieces.

26⅞″

Construct the front truss using two D pieces, four E pieces, and one G piece.

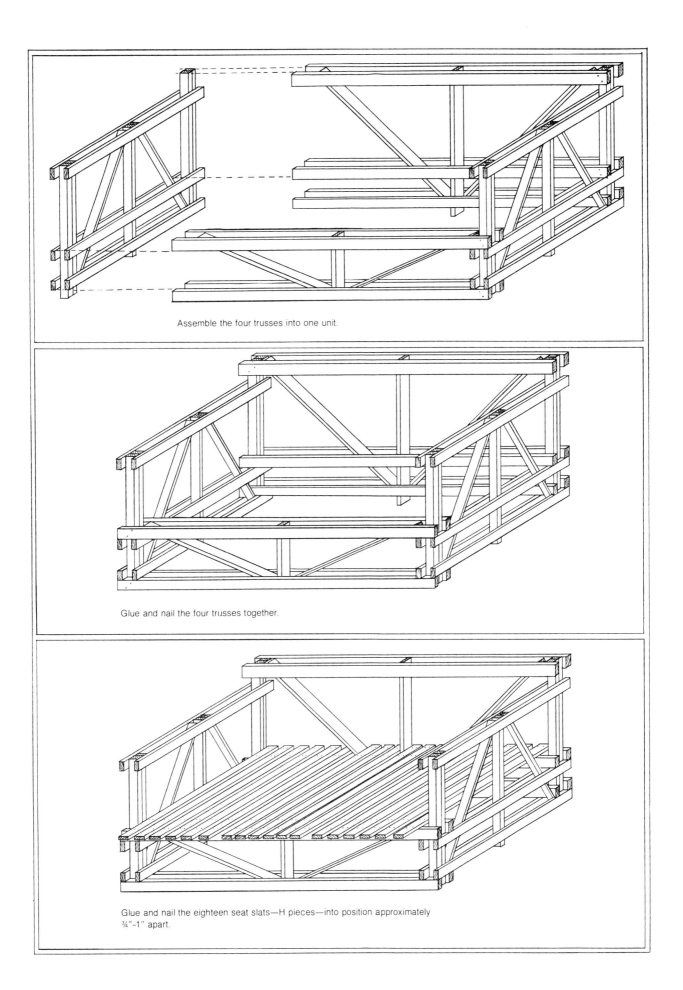

Assemble the four trusses into one unit.

Glue and nail the four trusses together.

Glue and nail the eighteen seat slats—H pieces—into position approximately ¾"-1" apart.

DESIGN 9

Sh'Matta 3   Designer: Stamberg

Piece	Section	Quantity	Length	Use
A	1″ × 2″	12	27″	side truss horizontals
B		8	22″	side truss front verticals & diagonals
C		2	21½″	side truss middle verticals
D		5	24″	side truss back verticals & rear truss vertical
E		10	78½″	front & rear truss horizontals
F		1	10½″	front truss vertical
G		2	37¼″	front truss diagonals
H		2	41½″	rear truss diagonals
I	1″ × 3″	20	30″	seat slats

For upholstery see pages 42 to 45.

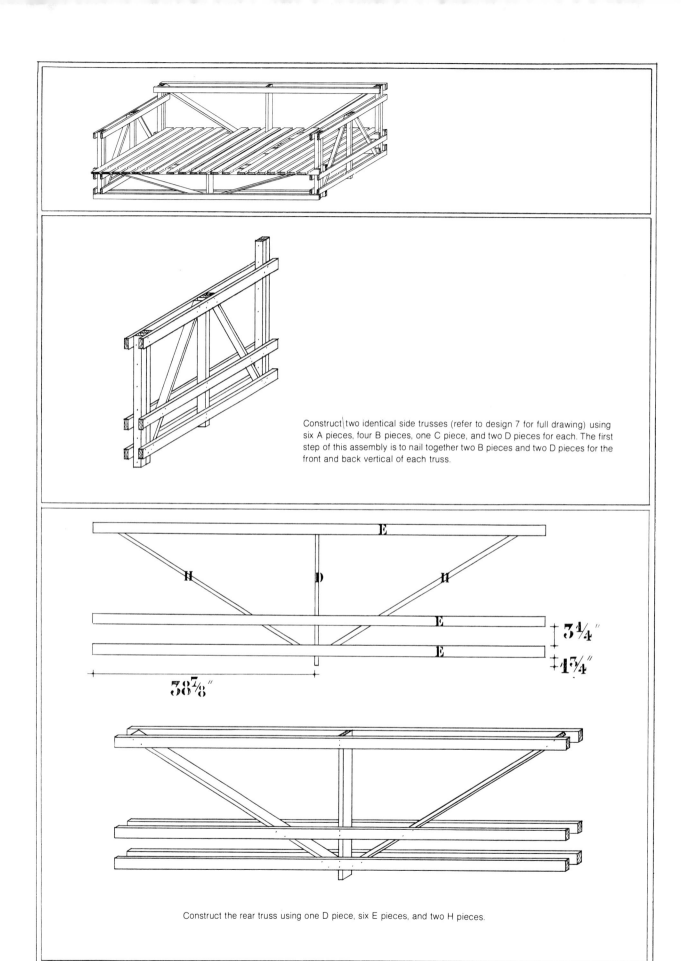

Construct two identical side trusses (refer to design 7 for full drawing) using six A pieces, four B pieces, one C piece, and two D pieces for each. The first step of this assembly is to nail together two B pieces and two D pieces for the front and back vertical of each truss.

E

H   D   H

E

E

$3\frac{1}{4}''$

$1\frac{3}{4}''$

$38\frac{7}{8}''$

Construct the rear truss using one D piece, six E pieces, and two H pieces.

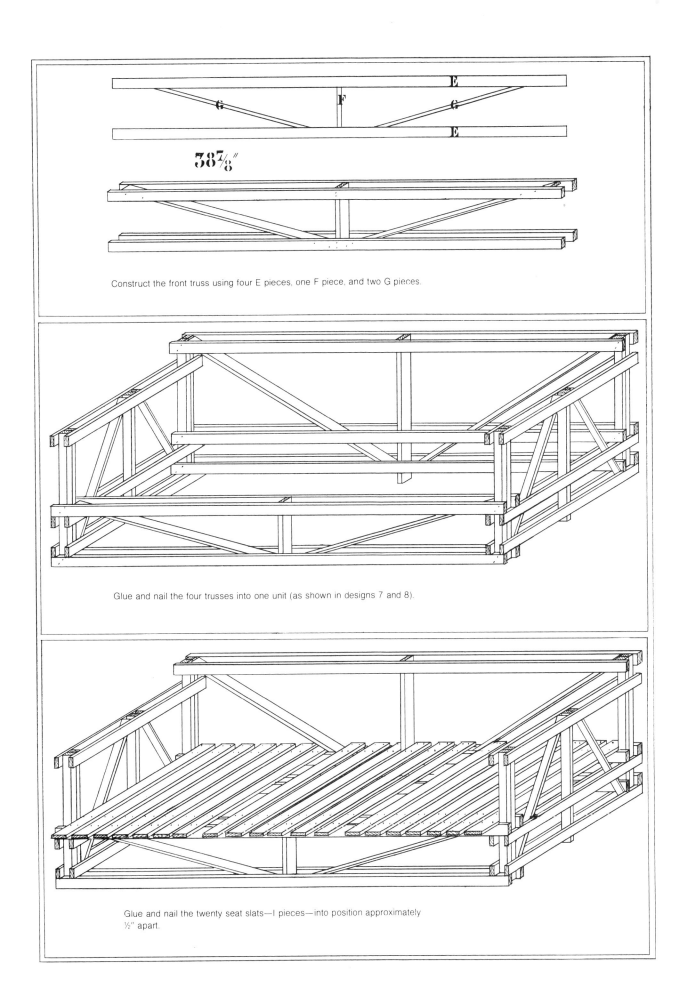

$38\frac{7}{8}''$

Construct the front truss using four E pieces, one F piece, and two G pieces.

Glue and nail the four trusses into one unit (as shown in designs 7 and 8).

Glue and nail the twenty seat slats—I pieces—into position approximately ½" apart.

DESIGN 10

Rabbit Chair   Designer: Stamberg

Piece	Section	Quantity	Length	Use
A	1″ × 2″	5	52″	back verticals & diagonals
B		10	13″	back horizontals
C		2	10″	back inside horizontals
D		8	16¼″	leg verticals & inside leg horizontals
E		2	18½″	leg diagonals
F		12	18″	leg horizontals
G		7	14½″	seat

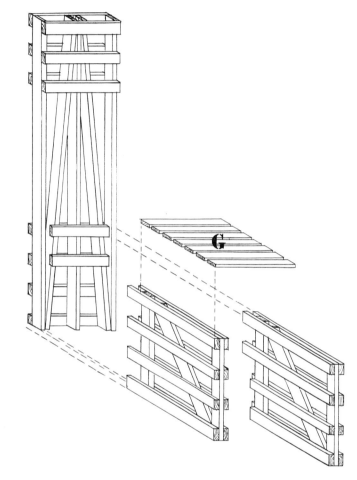

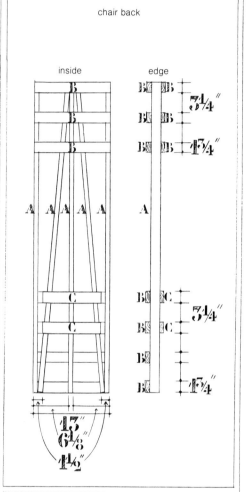

chair back

inside   edge

B   B   B

B   B   B   3¼"

B   B   B   1¾"

A A A A A   A

B   C

C   B   C   3¼"

C   B   C

B

B   1¾"

13"
6⅛"
1½"

After you construct the three basic enclosed trusses, simply silde the side trusses onto the edges—A pieces—of the back truss. Then drive one nail through each outside D piece into the A pieces and nail the seat slats into position. While you construct the side trusses, remember that they are not exactly the same but rather mirror images of each other.

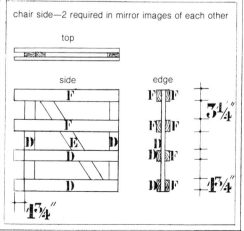

chair side—2 required in mirror images of each other

top

side   edge

F   F   F

F   F   F   3¼"

D   E   D   D   F

D   D   F

D   D   F   1¾"

1¾"

DESIGN II

JK   Designer: Stamberg

Piece	Section	Quantity	Length	Use
A	1″ × 2″	4	72″	diagonals
B		2	12″	bottom horizontals
C		16	24″	upper horizontals & shelf

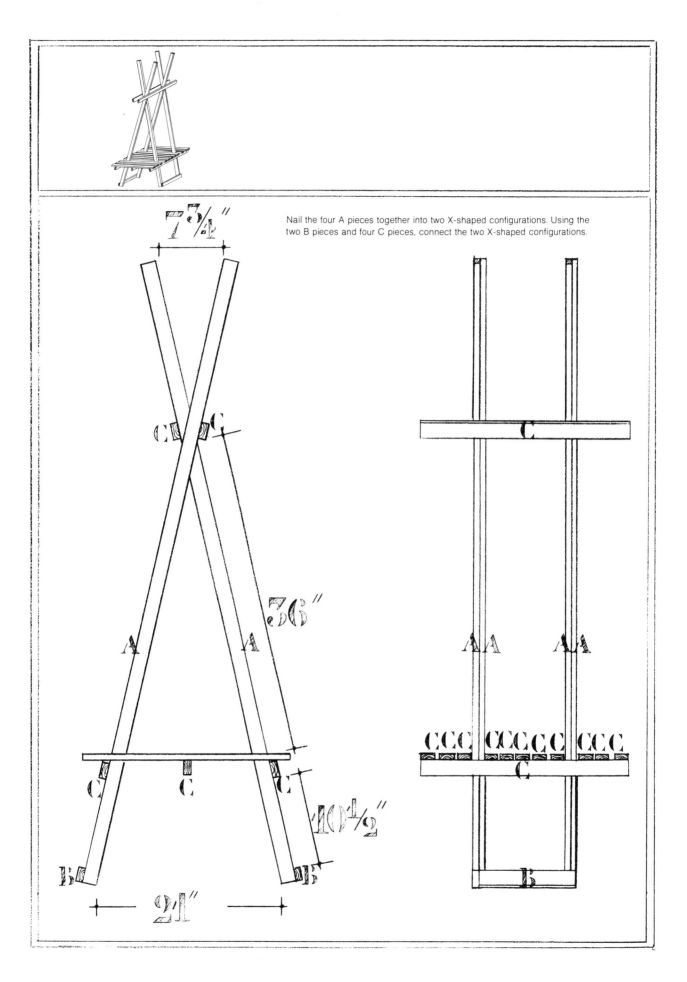

Nail the four A pieces together into two X-shaped configurations. Using the two B pieces and four C pieces, connect the two X-shaped configurations.

7 3/4"

36"

A   A

C   C

A   A

C

C   C

CCC   CCCC   CCC

C

10 1/2"

B   B

21"

B

Nail the shelf together as a separate unit. Use eleven C pieces for the shelf and one additional C piece as the central cross brace. Then simply rest the shelf on the lower C pieces of the rack.

DESIGN 12

Coop Desk   Designer: Stamberg

Piece	Section	Quantity	Length	Use
A	1" × 8"	4	61"	top
B	1" × 2"	36	26¾"	verticals
C		2	*28¼"	side truss top horizontals
D		2	*24"	side truss bottom horizontals
E		4	26"	side truss diagonals
F		3	59½"	front truss horizontals & top brace
G		2	35¼"	front truss diagonals

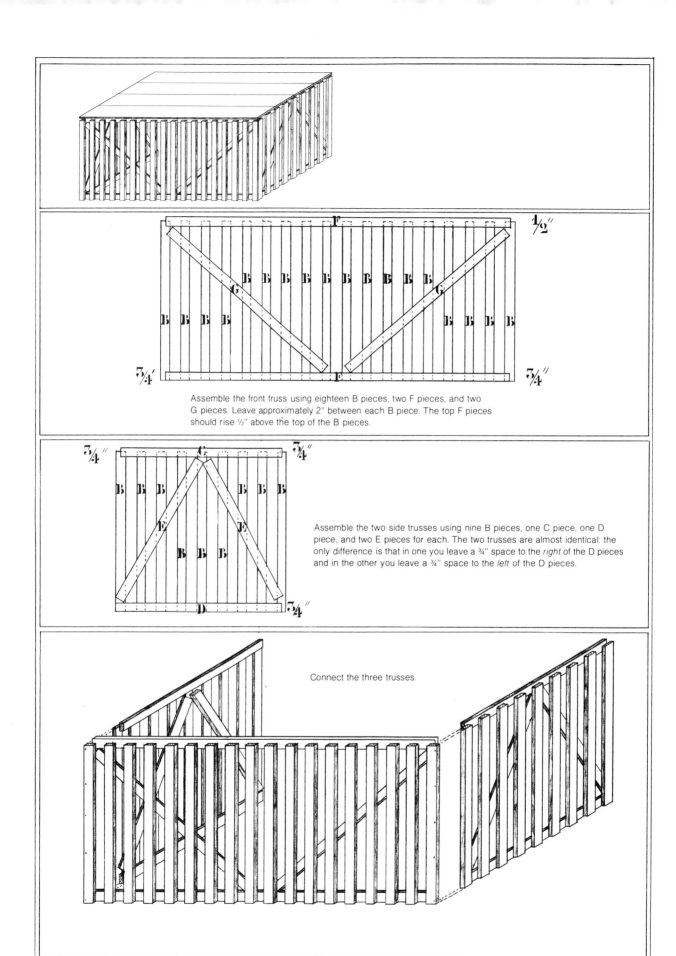

Assemble the front truss using eighteen B pieces, two F pieces, and two
G pieces. Leave approximately 2″ between each B piece. The top F pieces
should rise ½″ above the top of the B pieces.

Assemble the two side trusses using nine B pieces, one C piece, one D
piece, and two E pieces for each. The two trusses are almost identical: the
only difference is that in one you leave a ¾″ space to the *right* of the D pieces
and in the other you leave a ¾″ space to the *left* of the D pieces.

Connect the three trusses.

Attach the F brace into position.

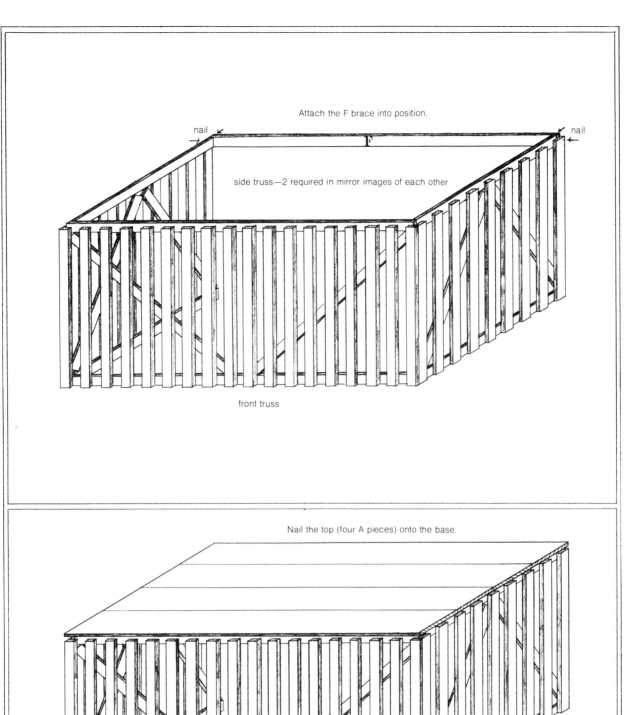

nail

nail

F

side truss—2 required in mirror images of each other

front truss

Nail the top (four A pieces) onto the base.

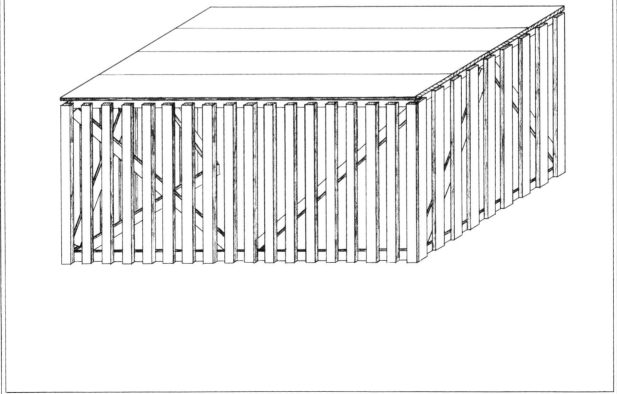

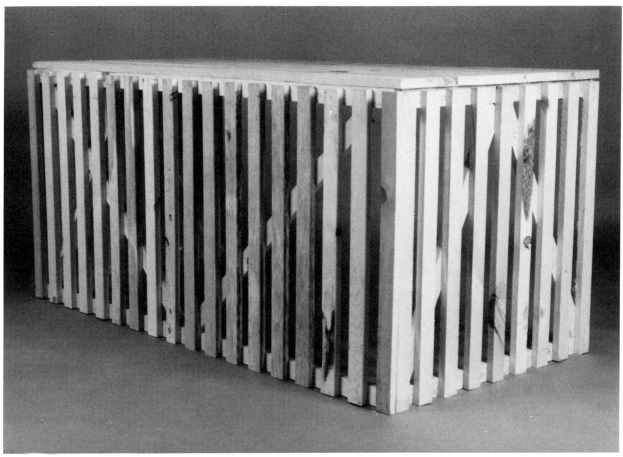

DESIGN 13

Queen Size Truss Bed   Designer: Stamberg

Piece	Section	Quantity	Length	Use
A	1″ × 2″	22	60″	low and high truss horizontals
B		9	9¾″	low & brace truss verticals
C		4	28″	low truss diagonals
D		3	17¾″	high truss verticals
E		2	32″	high truss diagonals
F		4	34¾″	brace truss horizontals
G		2	17″	brace truss diagonals
H		18	76¾″	platform slats

For this bed use a 4″ or 5″ high density foam mattress 60″ wide x 75″ long.

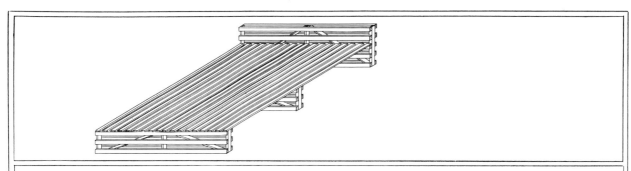

Assemble two identical low trusses using six A pieces, three B pieces, and two C pieces for each.

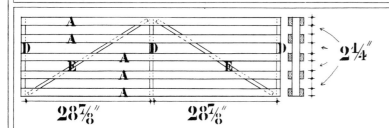

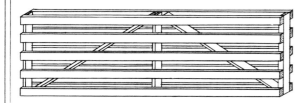

Assemble the high truss using ten A pieces, three D pieces, and two E pieces.

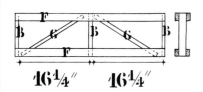

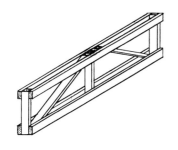

Assemble the brace truss using three B pieces, four F pieces, and two G pieces.

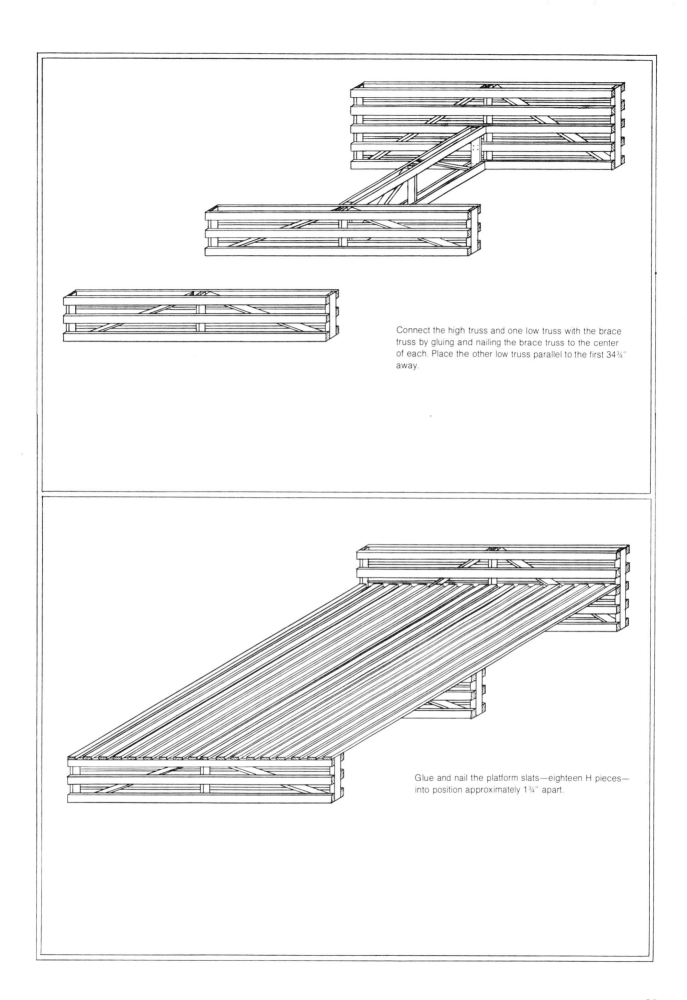

Connect the high truss and one low truss with the brace truss by gluing and nailing the brace truss to the center of each. Place the other low truss parallel to the first 34¾" away.

Glue and nail the platform slats—eighteen H pieces— into position approximately 1¾" apart.

DESIGN 14

AAJJ 1   Designer: Stamberg

Piece	Section	Quantity	Length	Use
A	1″ × 4″	15	52″	top
B		20	27¼″	base
C		4	*52″	top braces
D		4	*17½″	base braces
E		4	*14½″	base braces

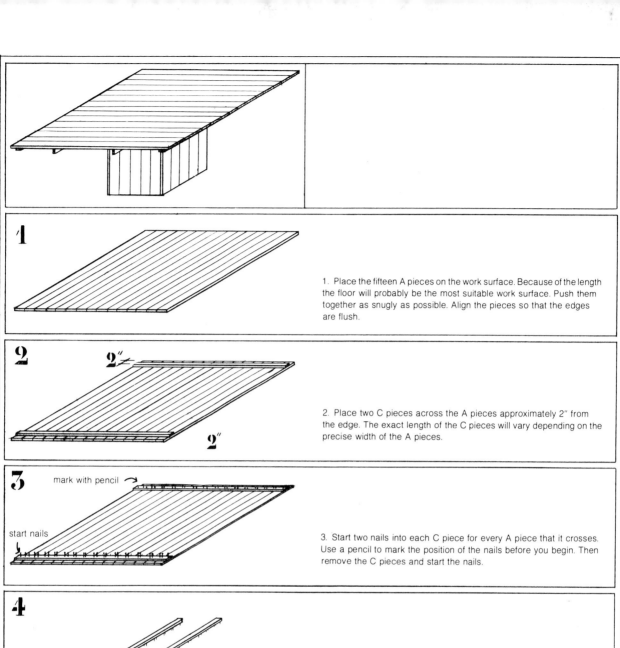

1

1. Place the fifteen A pieces on the work surface. Because of the length the floor will probably be the most suitable work surface. Push them together as snugly as possible. Align the pieces so that the edges are flush.

2

2″

2″

2. Place two C pieces across the A pieces approximately 2″ from the edge. The exact length of the C pieces will vary depending on the precise width of the A pieces.

3

mark with pencil

start nails

3. Start two nails into each C piece for every A piece that it crosses. Use a pencil to mark the position of the nails before you begin. Then remove the C pieces and start the nails.

4

block

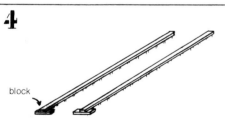

4. Turn the C pieces over and lay a line of glue on each. You should place a block under each piece to keep it from rocking or tilting while you apply the glue.

5

keep flush

5. Carefully align the A pieces. Replace the C pieces in position and drive the nails. Before starting each nail, check that the A pieces are in alignment.

6

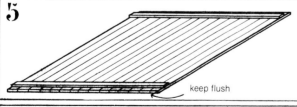

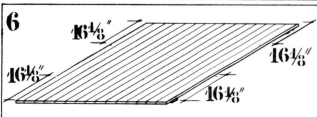

16⅛″

16⅛″

16⅛″

16⅛″

6. Turn over the slab you have just nailed together. From each corner measure 16⅛″ as shown and make small pencil marks. This dimension will vary according to the width of the wood used for the pedestal base. To calculate what this dimension should be, multiply the exact width of the B pieces by five. Add 2¼″. Subtract the sum from 52″. Divide by two. If the B pieces measure exactly 3½″, your measurement will be 16⅛″.

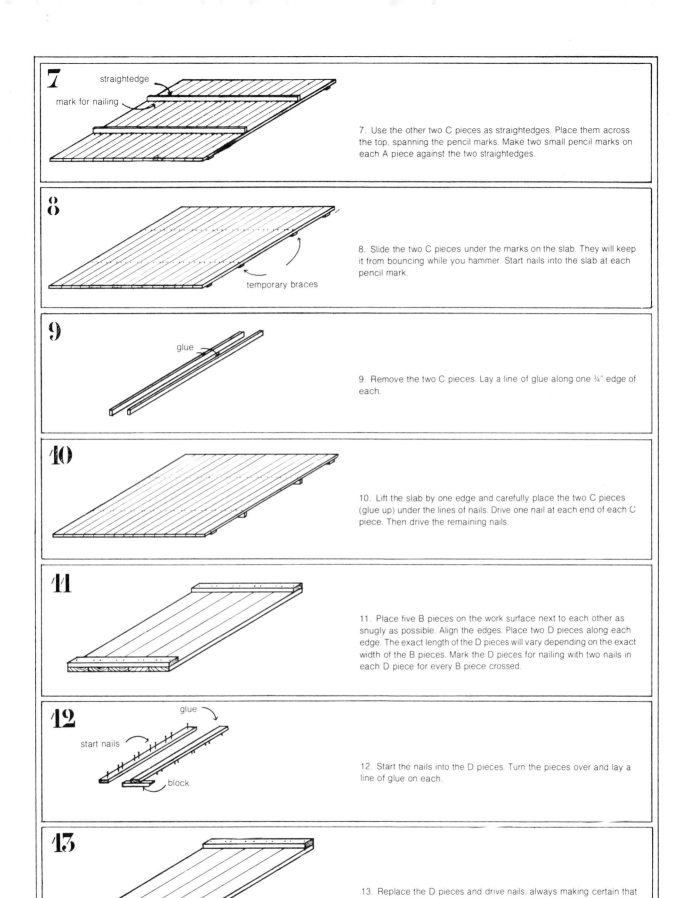

7 straightedge / mark for nailing

7. Use the other two C pieces as straightedges. Place them across the top, spanning the pencil marks. Make two small pencil marks on each A piece against the two straightedges.

8 temporary braces

8. Slide the two C pieces under the marks on the slab. They will keep it from bouncing while you hammer. Start nails into the slab at each pencil mark.

9 glue

9. Remove the two C pieces. Lay a line of glue along one ¾" edge of each.

10

10. Lift the slab by one edge and carefully place the two C pieces (glue up) under the lines of nails. Drive one nail at each end of each C piece. Then drive the remaining nails.

11

11. Place five B pieces on the work surface next to each other as snugly as possible. Align the edges. Place two D pieces along each edge. The exact length of the D pieces will vary depending on the exact width of the B pieces. Mark the D pieces for nailing with two nails in each D piece for every B piece crossed.

12 glue / start nails / block

12. Start the nails into the D pieces. Turn the pieces over and lay a line of glue on each.

13 keep flush

13. Replace the D pieces and drive nails, always making certain that the edge of the slab of B pieces is true.

14

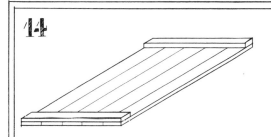

14. Repeat steps (11) through (13) to create another identical slab.

15

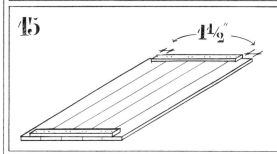

1½"

15. Place five B pieces on the work surface as in step (11). Then place two E pieces (the length will vary according to the exact width of the B pieces) on the edges so that they are 1½" from each long edge. Mark for nails.

16

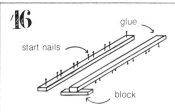

glue

start nails

block

16. Start the nails into each E piece. Turn them over and lay a line of glue on each.

17

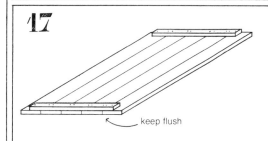

keep flush

17. Replace the E pieces and, keeping the edge true, drive the nails.

18

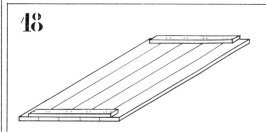

18. Repeat steps (15) through (17) to create an identical slab.

19

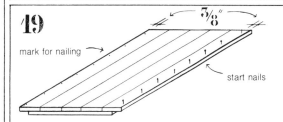

⅜"

mark for nailing

start nails

19. Start eight nails into each long edge of the two slabs created in steps (15) through (18). The nails should be ⅜" from the edge and about 3" apart.

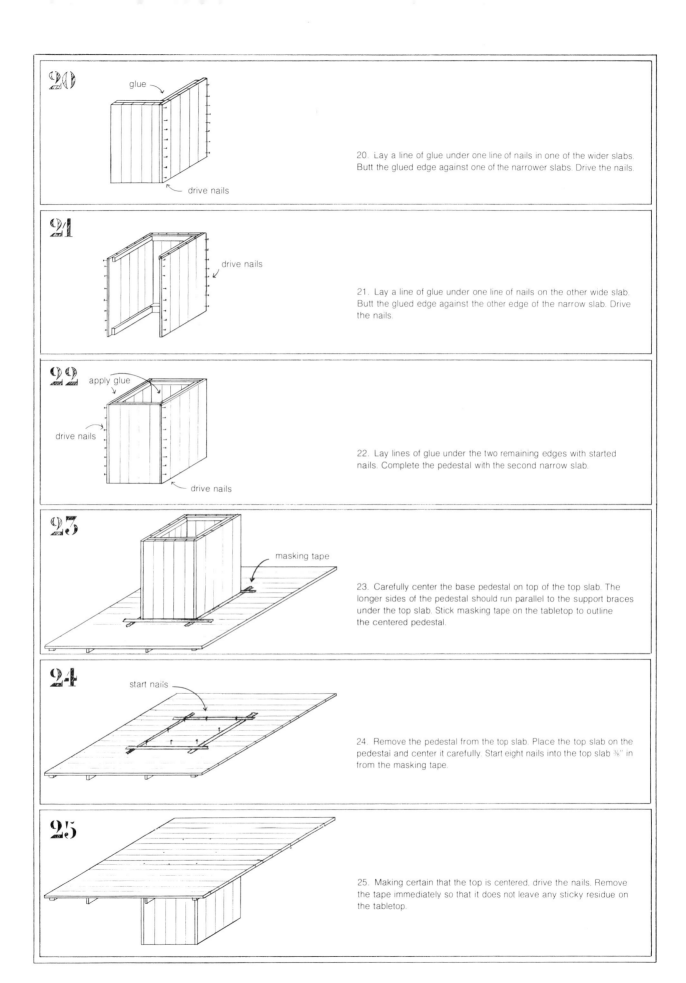

20. Lay a line of glue under one line of nails in one of the wider slabs. Butt the glued edge against one of the narrower slabs. Drive the nails.

21. Lay a line of glue under one line of nails on the other wide slab. Butt the glued edge against the other edge of the narrow slab. Drive the nails.

22. Lay lines of glue under the two remaining edges with started nails. Complete the pedestal with the second narrow slab.

23. Carefully center the base pedestal on top of the top slab. The longer sides of the pedestal should run parallel to the support braces under the top slab. Stick masking tape on the tabletop to outline the centered pedestal.

24. Remove the pedestal from the top slab. Place the top slab on the pedestal and center it carefully. Start eight nails into the top slab ⅜" in from the masking tape.

25. Making certain that the top is centered, drive the nails. Remove the tape immediately so that it does not leave any sticky residue on the tabletop.

DESIGN 15

AAJJ 2   Designer: Stamberg

Piece	Section	Quantity	Length	Use
A	1″ × 4″	13	94″	tabletop
B		40	27¼″	pedestal verticals
C	1″ × 2″	6	*45″	tabletop braces
D		8	*17½″	pedestal braces
E		8	*14½″	pedestal braces

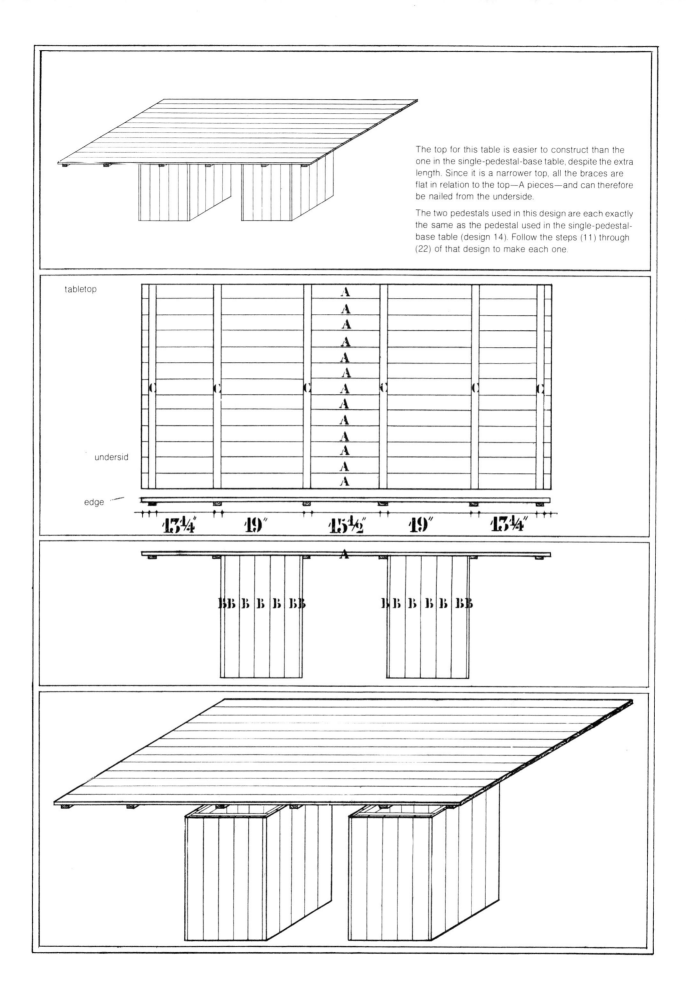

The top for this table is easier to construct than the one in the single-pedestal-base table, despite the extra length. Since it is a narrower top, all the braces are flat in relation to the top—A pieces—and can therefore be nailed from the underside.

The two pedestals used in this design are each exactly the same as the pedestal used in the single-pedestal-base table (design 14). Follow the steps (11) through (22) of that design to make each one.

tabletop

A
A
A
A
A
A
A
A
A
A
A
A

C   C   C   C   C   C

undersid

edge

13¼″   19″   15½″   19″   13¼″

A

BB B B B BB   BB B B B BB

DESIGN 16

AAJJ 3   Designer: Stamberg

Piece	Section	Quantity	Length	Use
A	1″ × 4″	14	*49″	top
B		28	16½″	sides
C	1″ × 2″	4	*47″	top braces
D		4	*24½″	side horizontals
E		4	*21½″	side horizontals

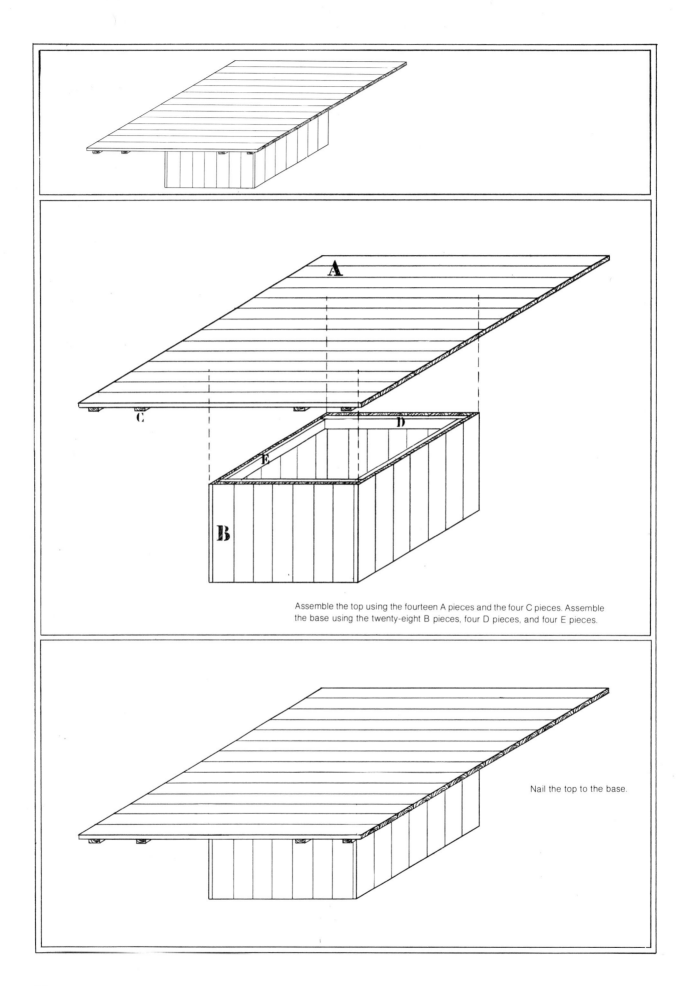

Assemble the top using the fourteen A pieces and the four C pieces. Assemble the base using the twenty-eight B pieces, four D pieces, and four E pieces.

Nail the top to the base.

DESIGN 17

Box Table   Designer: Stamberg

Piece	Section	Quantity	Length	Use
A	1″ × 4″	28	16¼″	side verticals
B		7	*26″	top
C	1″ × 2″	4	*24½″	side horizontals
D		4	*21½″	side horizontals

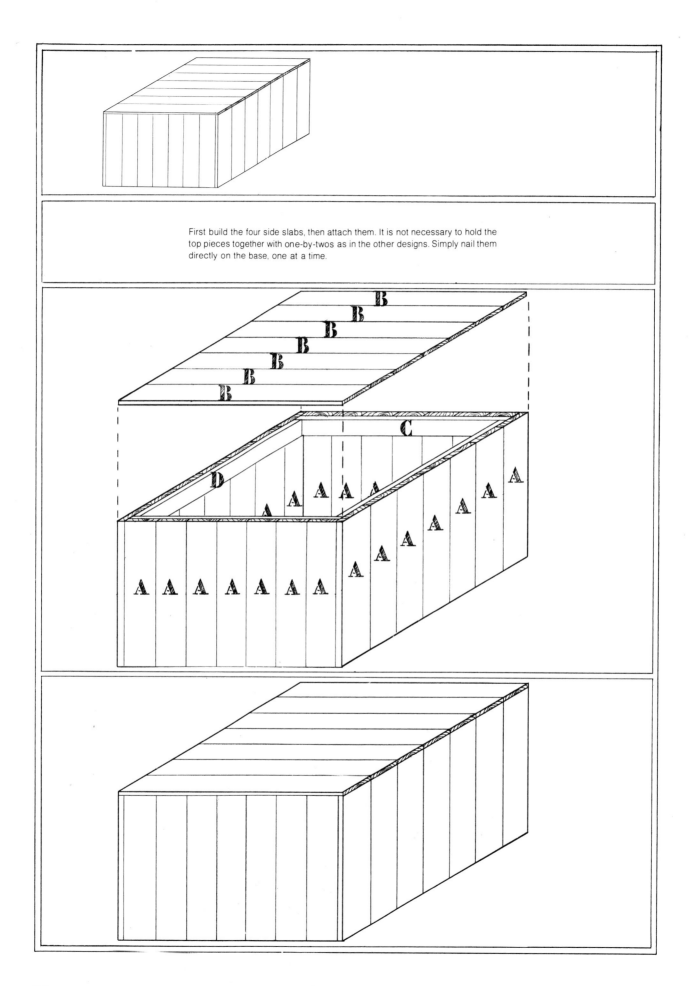

First build the four side slabs, then attach them. It is not necessary to hold the top pieces together with one-by-twos as in the other designs. Simply nail them directly on the base, one at a time.

DESIGN 18

EMME Single   Designer: Enzo Mari

Piece	Section	Quantity	Length	Use
A	1″ × 4″	2	35½″	headboard & footboard horizontals
B		1	28½″	headboard horizontal
C		3	21½″	headboard horizontal & diagonals
D		1	14½″	headboard horizontal
E		8	10½″	headboard, footboard, & sideboard horizontals
F		4	*10½″	headboard & footboard verticals
G		4	8½″	headboard horizontals & footboard verticals
H		6	7″	footboard & sideboard horizontals
I		2	78″	sideboard horizontals
J		2	*8″	sideboard verticals
K	1″ × 2″	2	75″	sideboard horizontals
L		30	35½″	platform slats

For this bed use a high density foam mattress 4″ thick x 36″ wide x 75″ long.

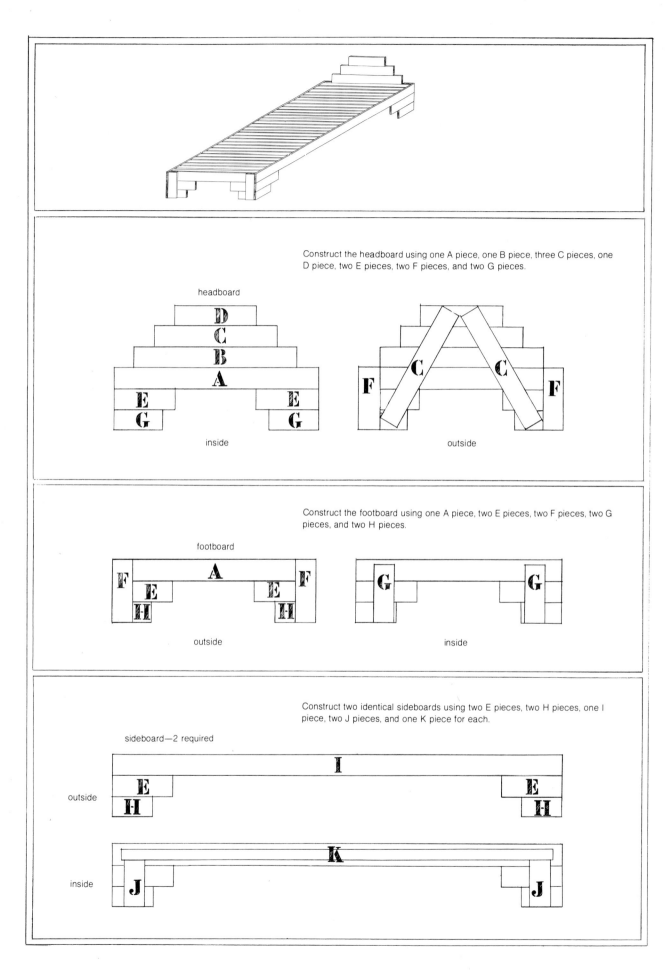

Construct the headboard using one A piece, one B piece, three C pieces, one D piece, two E pieces, two F pieces, and two G pieces.

headboard

inside

outside

Construct the footboard using one A piece, two E pieces, two F pieces, two G pieces, and two H pieces.

footboard

outside

inside

Construct two identical sideboards using two E pieces, two H pieces, one I piece, two J pieces, and one K piece for each.

sideboard—2 required

outside

inside

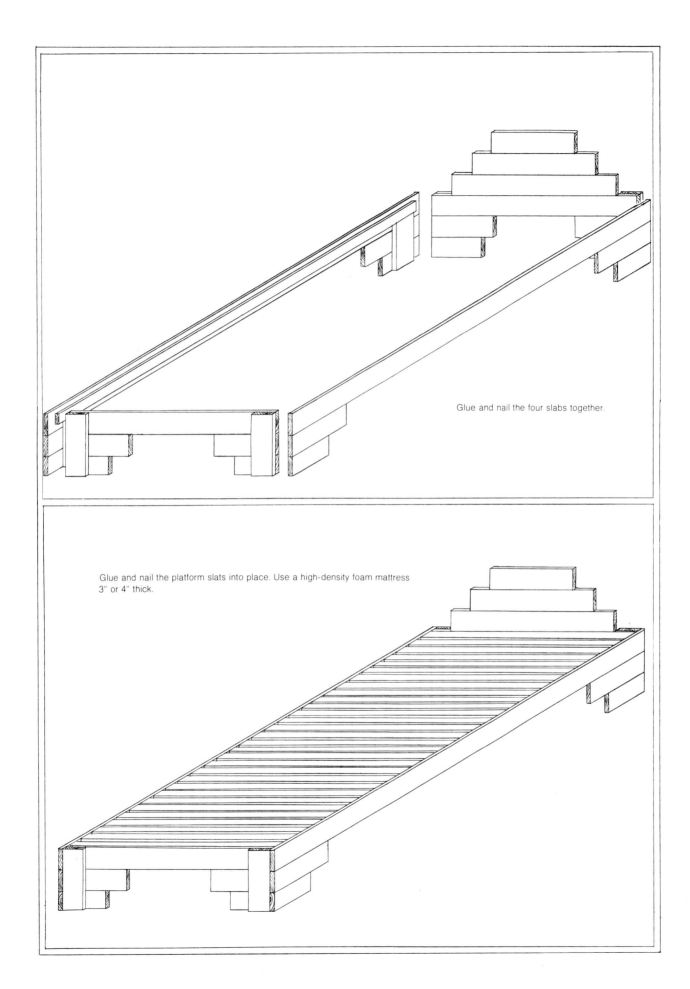

Glue and nail the four slabs together.

Glue and nail the platform slats into place. Use a high-density foam mattress 3″ or 4″ thick.

DESIGN 19

EMME Double   Designer: Enzo Mari

Piece	Section	Quantity	Length	Use
A	1″ × 4″	2	53½″	headboard & footboard horizontals
B		1	42″	headboard horizontal
C		1	30″	headboard horizontal
D		5	18″	headboard & footboard horizontals
E		2	25″	headboard diagonals
F		4	12″	headboard & footboard horizontals
G		2	14″	footboard diagonals
H		4	*10½″	headboard & footboard verticals
I		2	78″	sideboard horizontals
J		4	7″	sideboard horizontals
K		4	10½″	sideboard horizontals
L		4	*8¾″	sideboard verticals
M	1″ × 2″	2	68″	sideboard horizontals
N		45	53½″	platform slats

For this bed use a high density foam mattress 4″ thick x 54″ wide x 75″ long.

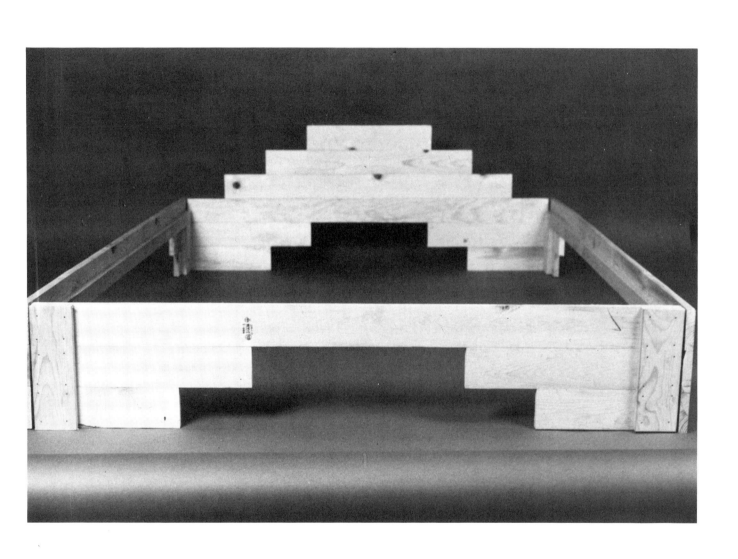

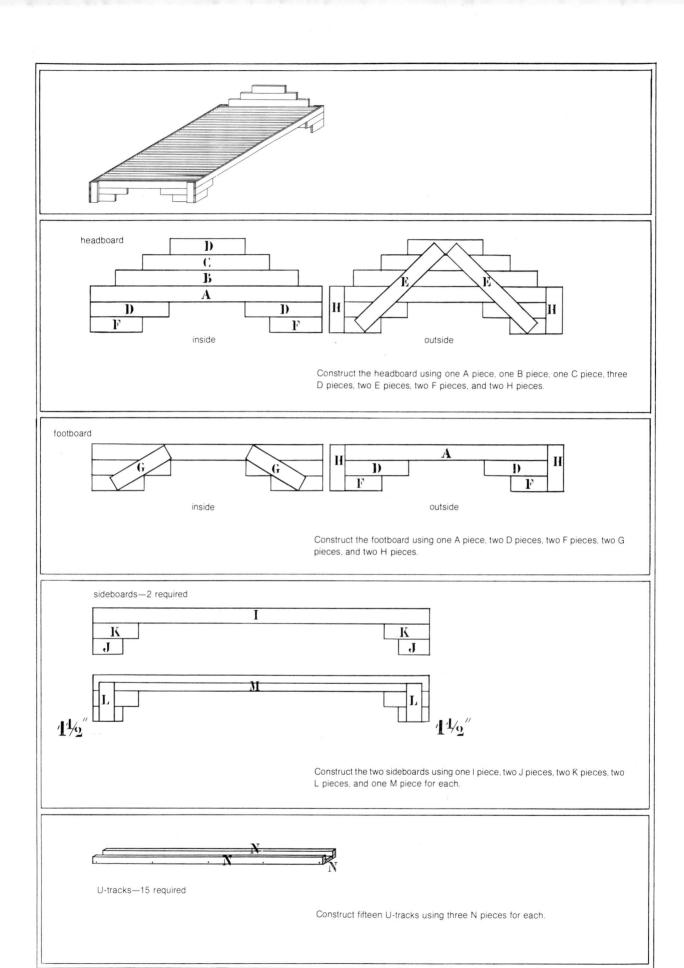

headboard

inside

outside

Construct the headboard using one A piece, one B piece, one C piece, three D pieces, two E pieces, two F pieces, and two H pieces.

footboard

inside

outside

Construct the footboard using one A piece, two D pieces, two F pieces, two G pieces, and two H pieces.

sideboards—2 required

1½″   1½″

Construct the two sideboards using one I piece, two J pieces, two K pieces, two L pieces, and one M piece for each.

U-tracks—15 required

Construct fifteen U-tracks using three N pieces for each.

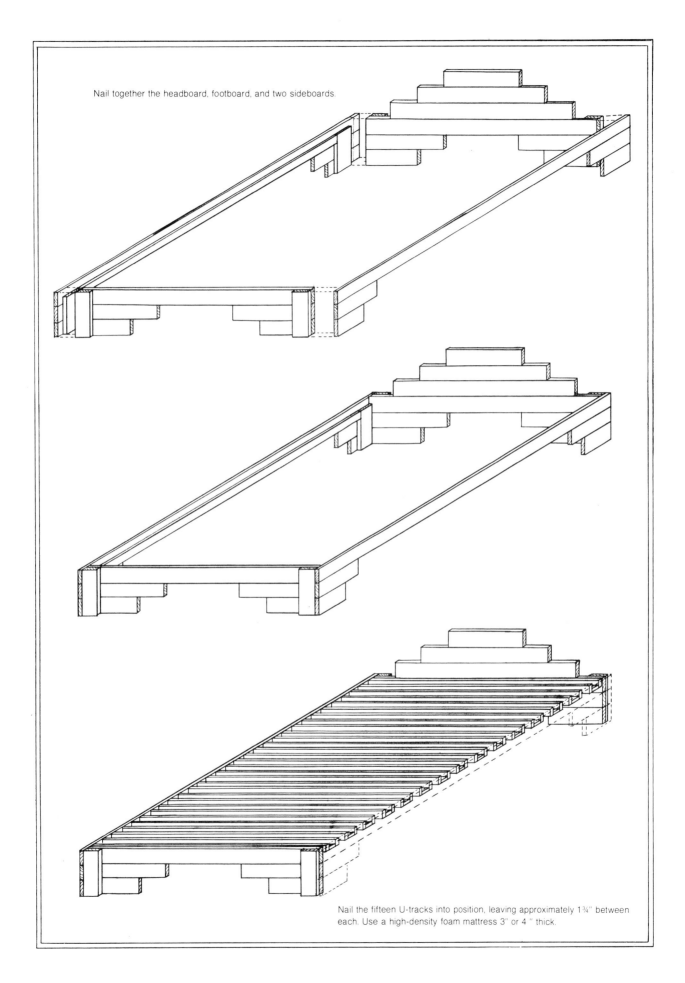

Nail together the headboard, footboard, and two sideboards.

Nail the fifteen U-tracks into position, leaving approximately 1¾" between each. Use a high-density foam mattress 3" or 4 " thick.

Cardinal Dots   Designer: Stamberg

Piece	Section	Quantity	Length	Use
A	1″ × 3″	14	24″	sides & back
B		5	37″	back
C		6	*16″	seat
D	1″ × 2″	1	*17½″	bottom back horizontal
E		1	*12½″	middle back horizontal
F		1	*7½″	top back horizontal
G		2	11½″	back diagonal
H		2	*15¾″	arms
I		2	*15″	side braces
J		1	*16″	rear seat support
K		4	*14¼″	side seat braces

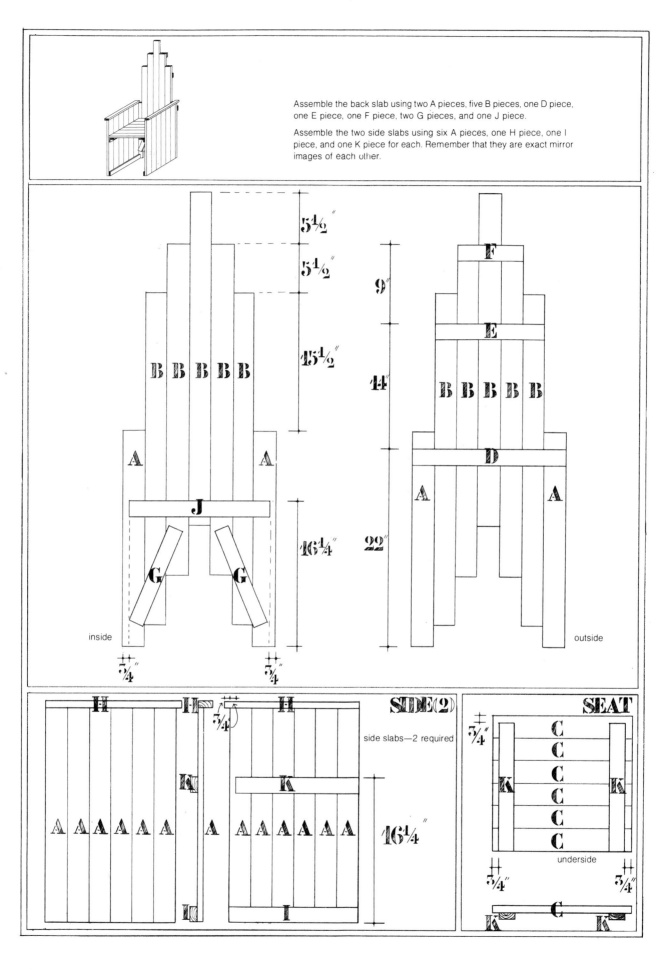

Assemble the back slab using two A pieces, five B pieces, one D piece, one E piece, one F piece, two G pieces, and one J piece.

Assemble the two side slabs using six A pieces, one H piece, one I piece, and one K piece for each. Remember that they are exact mirror images of each other.

5½″

5½″

45½″

16¼″

9″

44″

22″

B B B B B

A   A

J

G   G

inside

¾″   ¾″

F

E

B B B B B

D

A   A

outside

H   H   H

¾″

H

SIDE(2)

side slabs—2 required

K

K

16¼″

A A A A A A

A A A A A A

I

I

SEAT

¾″

C
C
C
C
C
C

K   K

underside

¾″   ¾″

C

K   K

96

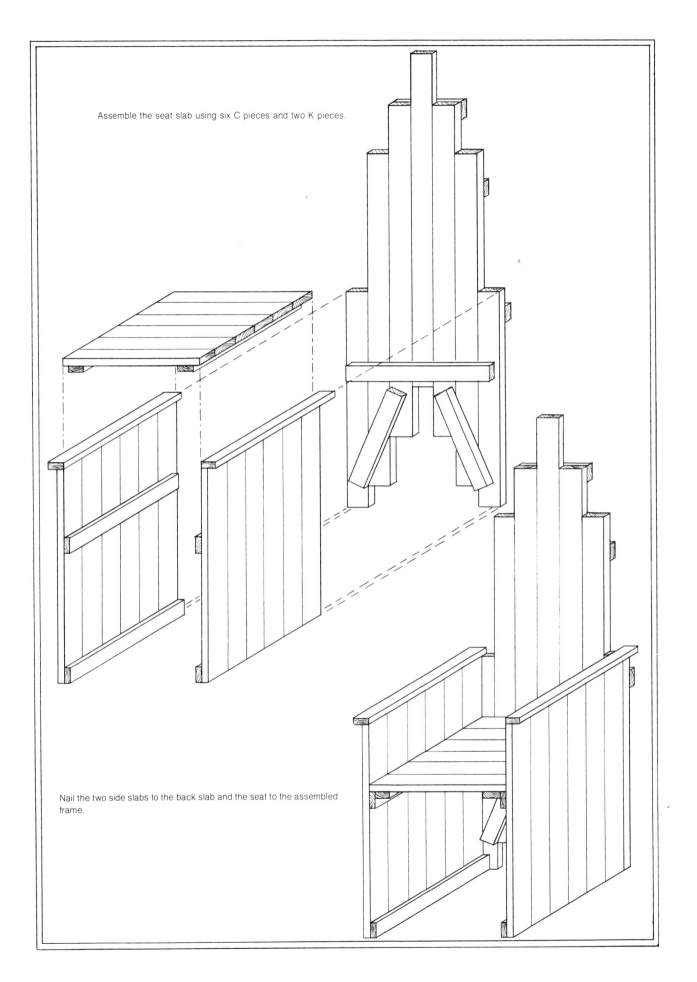

Assemble the seat slab using six C pieces and two K pieces.

Nail the two side slabs to the back slab and the seat to the assembled frame.

DESIGN 21

JSJ   Designer: Stamberg

Piece	Section	Quantity	Length	Use
A	1″ × 6″	2	44″	back vertical
B		3	17″	seat
C		4	16¼″	leg vertical
D	1″ × 4″	1	18″	back vertical
E	1″ × 2″	2	15″	bottom leg horizontals
F		3	15½″	back horizontals
G		2	16″	top leg horizontals

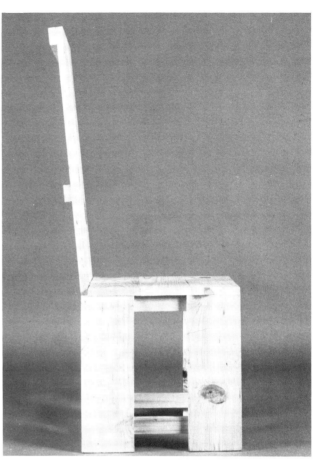

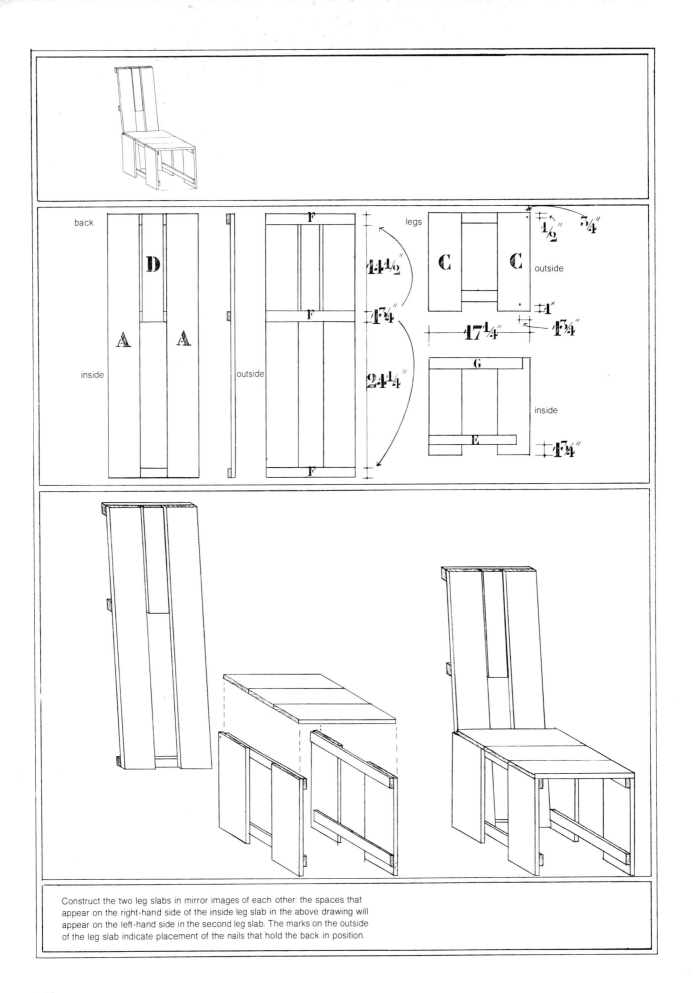

back

D

A   A

inside   outside

F

F

F

legs

C   C

outside

G

inside

E

$44\frac{1}{2}''$

$7\frac{1}{4}''$

$24\frac{1}{4}''$

$\frac{1}{2}''$ $\frac{3}{4}''$

$1''$

$17\frac{1}{4}''$ $1\frac{3}{4}''$

$1\frac{3}{4}''$

Construct the two leg slabs in mirror images of each other: the spaces that
appear on the right-hand side of the inside leg slab in the above drawing will
appear on the left-hand side in the second leg slab. The marks on the outside
of the leg slab indicate placement of the nails that hold the back in position.

DESIGN 22

MS   Designer: Stamberg

Piece	Section	Quantity	Length	Use
A	1″ × 6″	16	27¼″	legs
B		6	72″	top
C	1″ × 2″	3	*33″	top braces

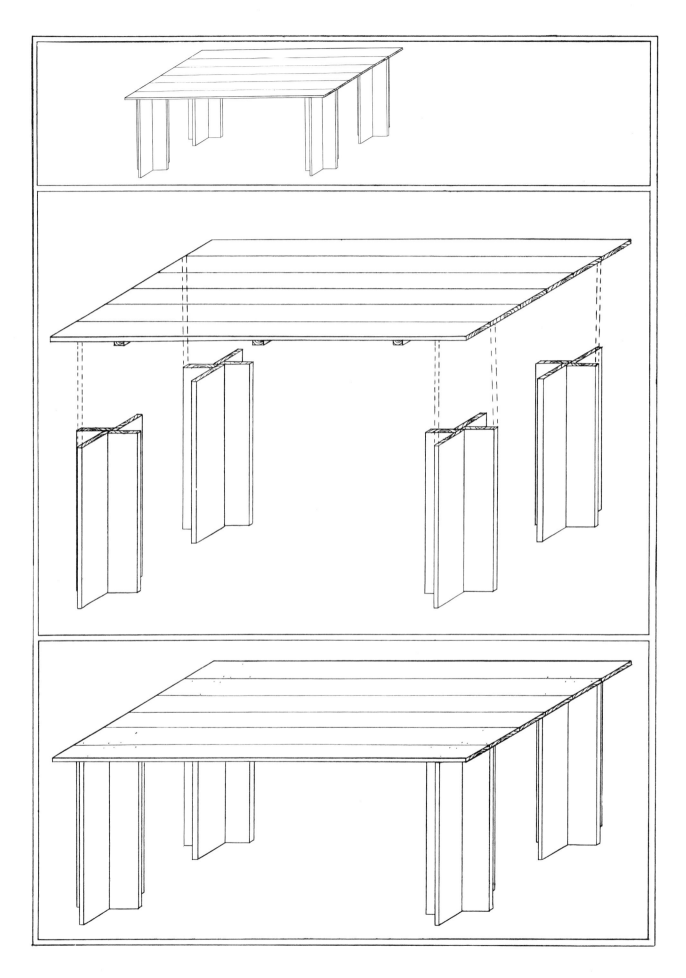

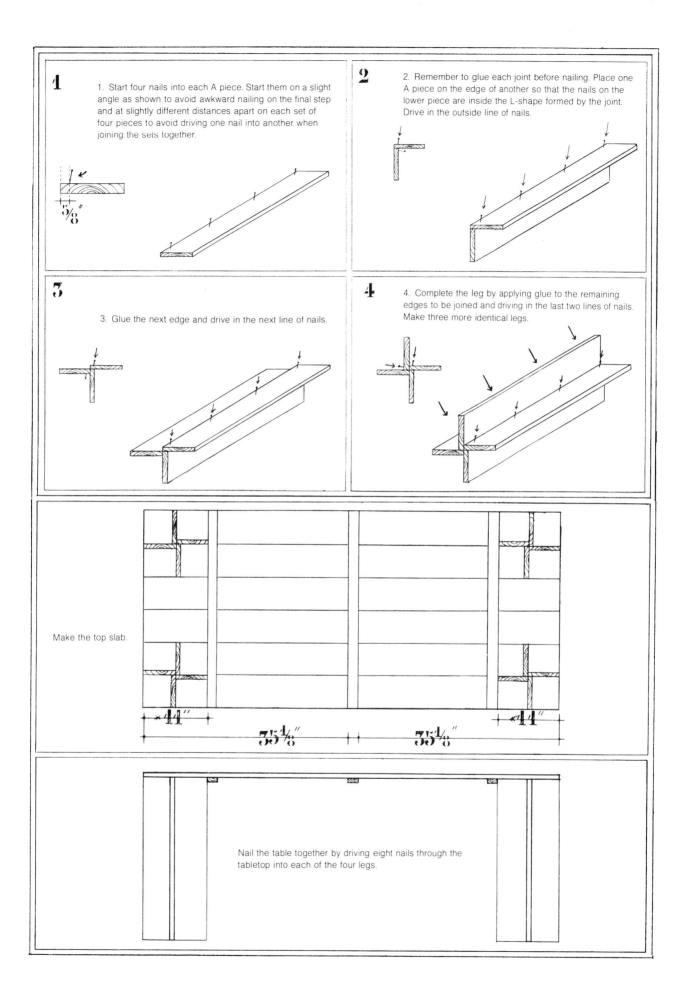

1

1. Start four nails into each A piece. Start them on a slight angle as shown to avoid awkward nailing on the final step and at slightly different distances apart on each set of four pieces to avoid driving one nail into another when joining the sets together.

⅝"

2

2. Remember to glue each joint before nailing. Place one A piece on the edge of another so that the nails on the lower piece are inside the L-shape formed by the joint. Drive in the outside line of nails.

3

3. Glue the next edge and drive in the next line of nails.

4

4. Complete the leg by applying glue to the remaining edges to be joined and driving in the last two lines of nails. Make three more identical legs.

Make the top slab.

4" 35⅛" 35⅛" 4"

Nail the table together by driving eight nails through the tabletop into each of the four legs.

DESIGN 23

LS   Designer: Stamberg

Piece	Section	Quantity	Length	Use
A	1″ × 6″	16	16¼″	legs
B		7	38½″	top
C	1″ × 2″	2	*38½″	top braces

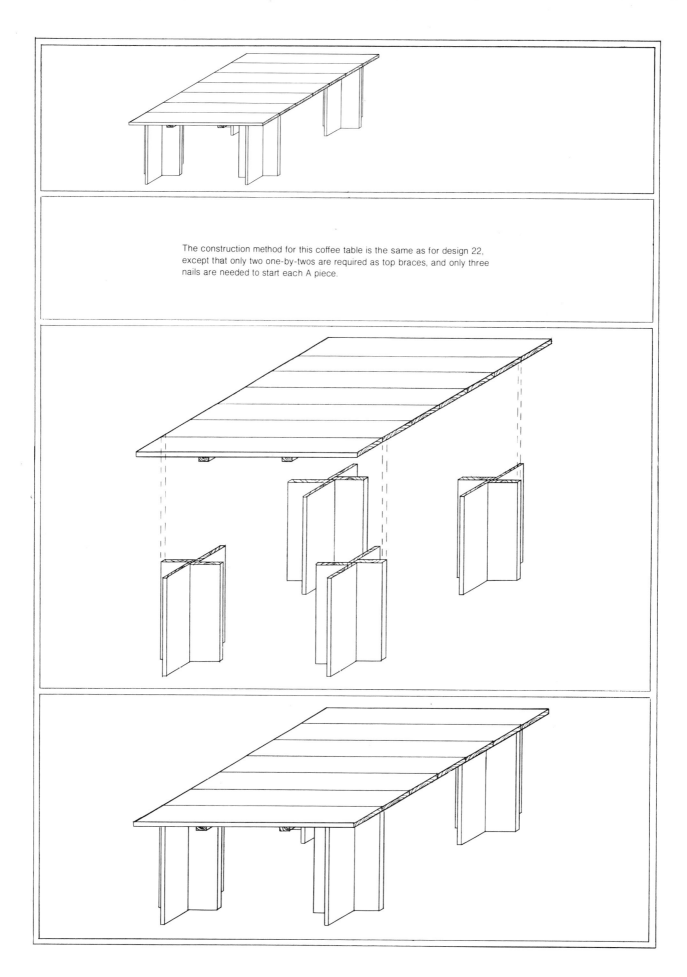

The construction method for this coffee table is the same as for design 22, except that only two one-by-twos are required as top braces, and only three nails are needed to start each A piece.

Crate 2   Designer: Gerrit T. Rietveld

Piece	Section	Quantity	Length	Use
A	1″ × 6″	6	23½″	top and leg horizontals
B		4	17″	legs
C	1″ × 3″	2	23½″	top braces

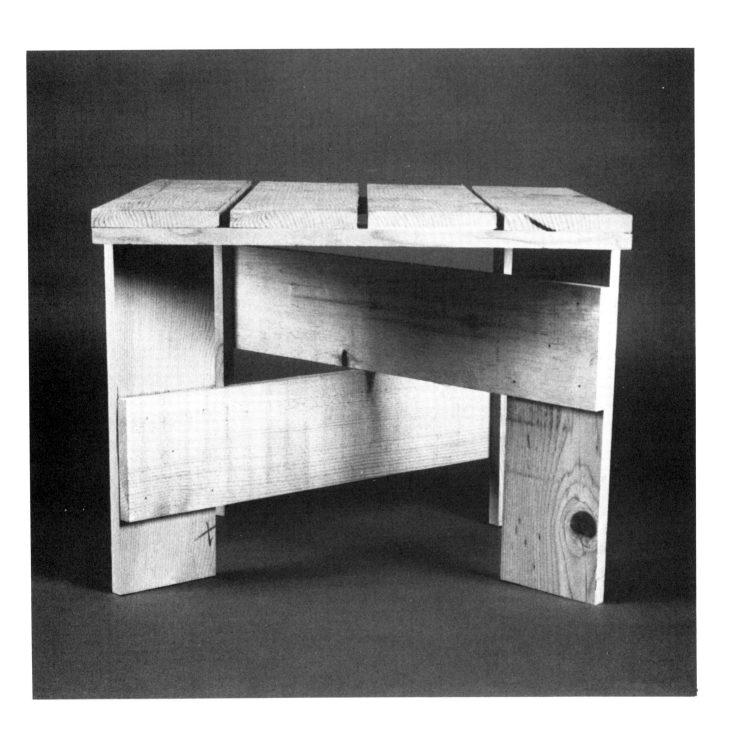

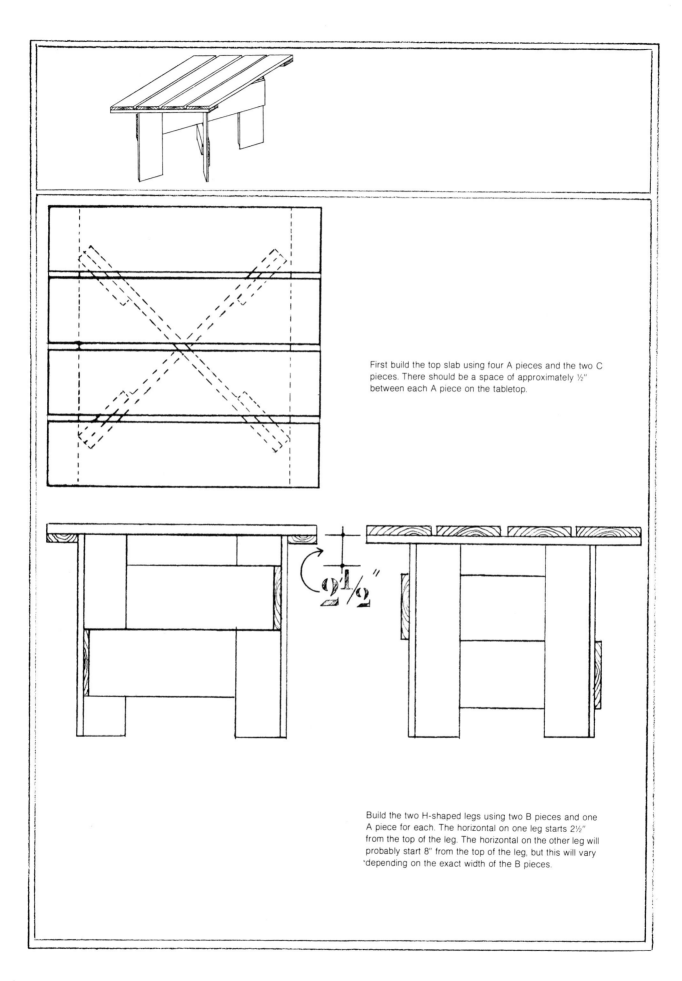

First build the top slab using four A pieces and the two C pieces. There should be a space of approximately ½″ between each A piece on the tabletop.

2½″

Build the two H-shaped legs using two B pieces and one A piece for each. The horizontal on one leg starts 2½″ from the top of the leg. The horizontal on the other leg will probably start 8″ from the top of the leg, but this will vary depending on the exact width of the B pieces.

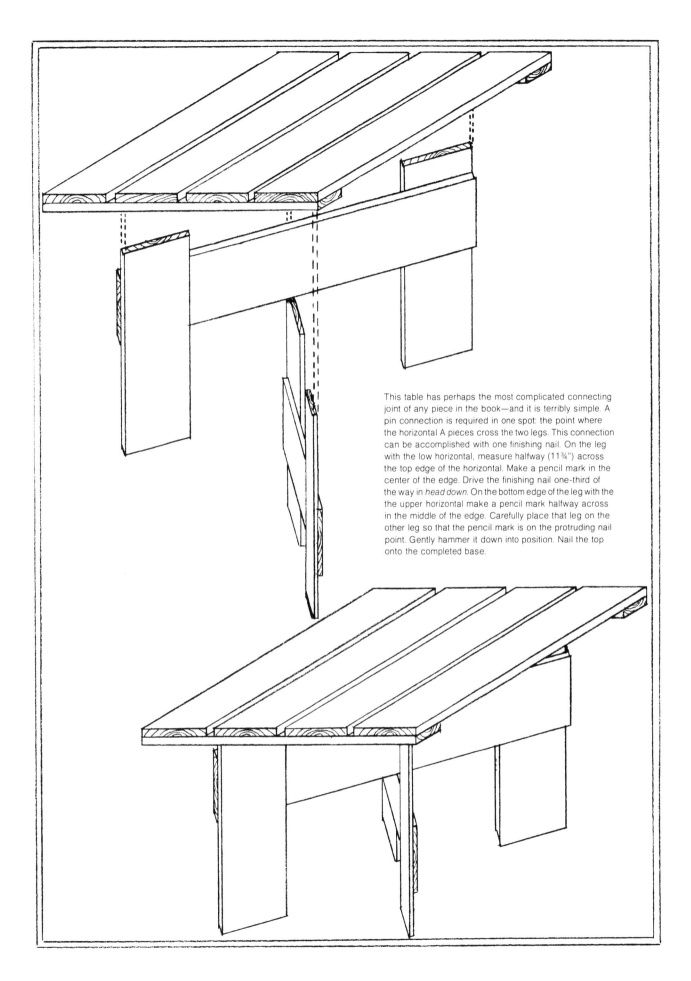

This table has perhaps the most complicated connecting joint of any piece in the book—and it is terribly simple. A pin connection is required in one spot: the point where the horizontal A pieces cross the two legs. This connection can be accomplished with one finishing nail. On the leg with the low horizontal, measure halfway (11¾") across the top edge of the horizontal. Make a pencil mark in the center of the edge. Drive the finishing nail one-third of the way in *head down*. On the bottom edge of the leg with the the upper horizontal make a pencil mark halfway across in the middle of the edge. Carefully place that leg on the other leg so that the pencil mark is on the protruding nail point. Gently hammer it down into position. Nail the top onto the completed base.

Crate 3   Designer: Gerrit T. Rietveld

Piece	Section	Quantity	Length	Use
A	1″×10″	9	48½″	shelves & side verticals

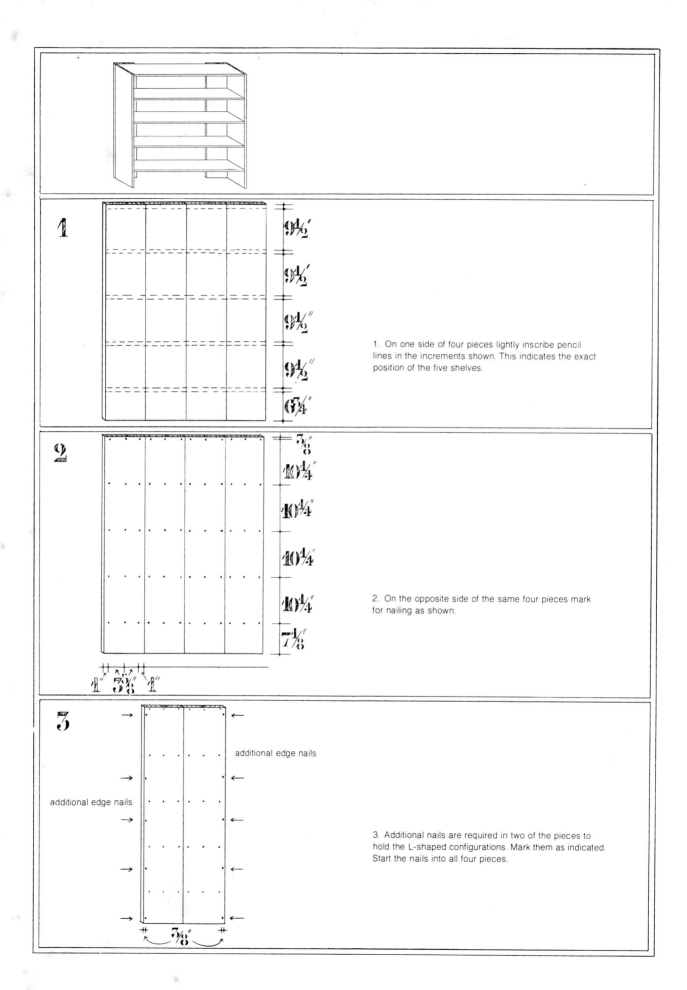

1

9½"

9½"

9½"

9½"

6¾"

1. On one side of four pieces lightly inscribe pencil lines in the increments shown. This indicates the exact position of the five shelves.

2

⅜"

10¼"

10¼"

10¼"

10¼"

7⅛"

1" 5⅝" 1"

2. On the opposite side of the same four pieces mark for nailing as shown.

3

additional edge nails

additional edge nails

5⅝"

3. Additional nails are required in two of the pieces to hold the L-shaped configurations. Mark them as indicated. Start the nails into all four pieces.

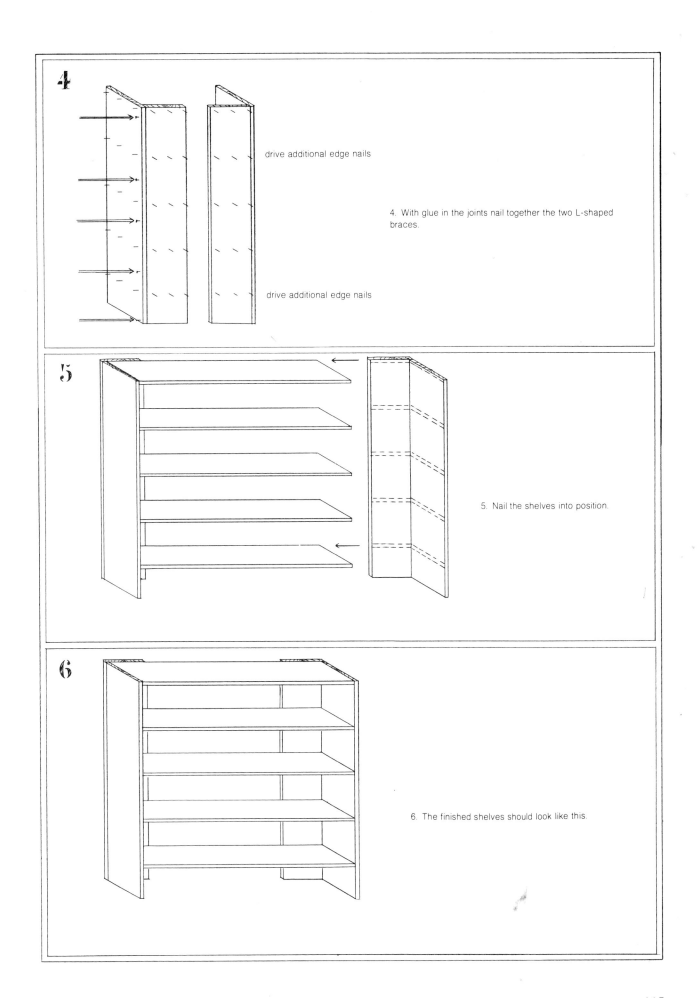

drive additional edge nails

4. With glue in the joints nail together the two L-shaped braces.

drive additional edge nails

5. Nail the shelves into position.

6. The finished shelves should look like this.

DESIGN 26

Crate 6   Designer: Gerrit T. Rietveld

Piece	Section	Quantity	Length	Use
A	1″ × 6″	10	17½″	shelves & legs
B	1″ × 3″	4	17½″	shelf supports

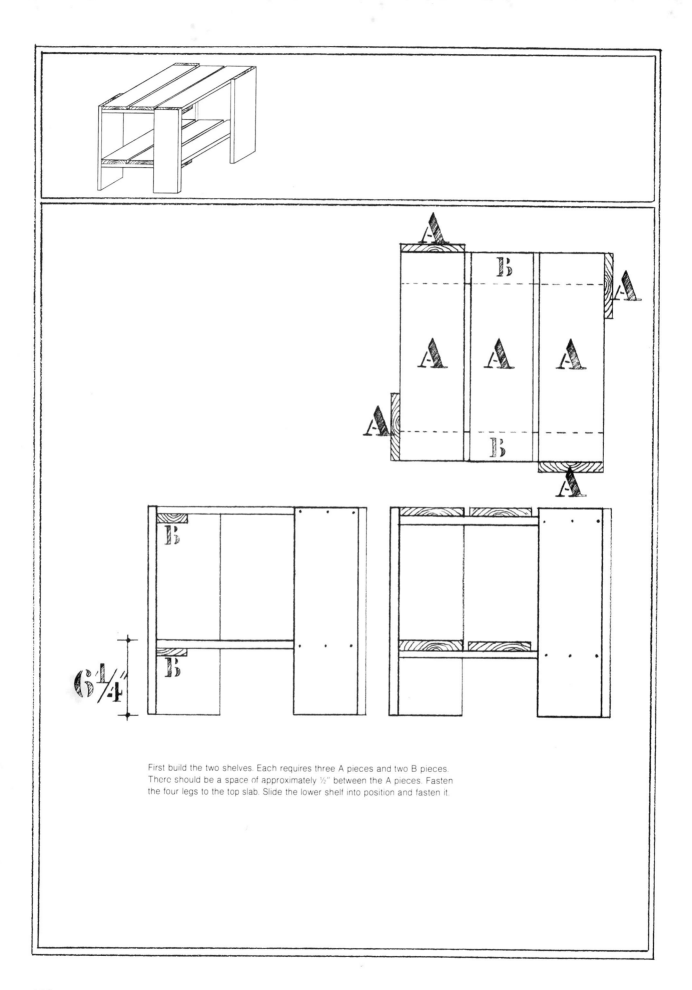

First build the two shelves. Each requires three A pieces and two B pieces. There should be a space of approximately ½" between the A pieces. Fasten the four legs to the top slab. Slide the lower shelf into position and fasten it.

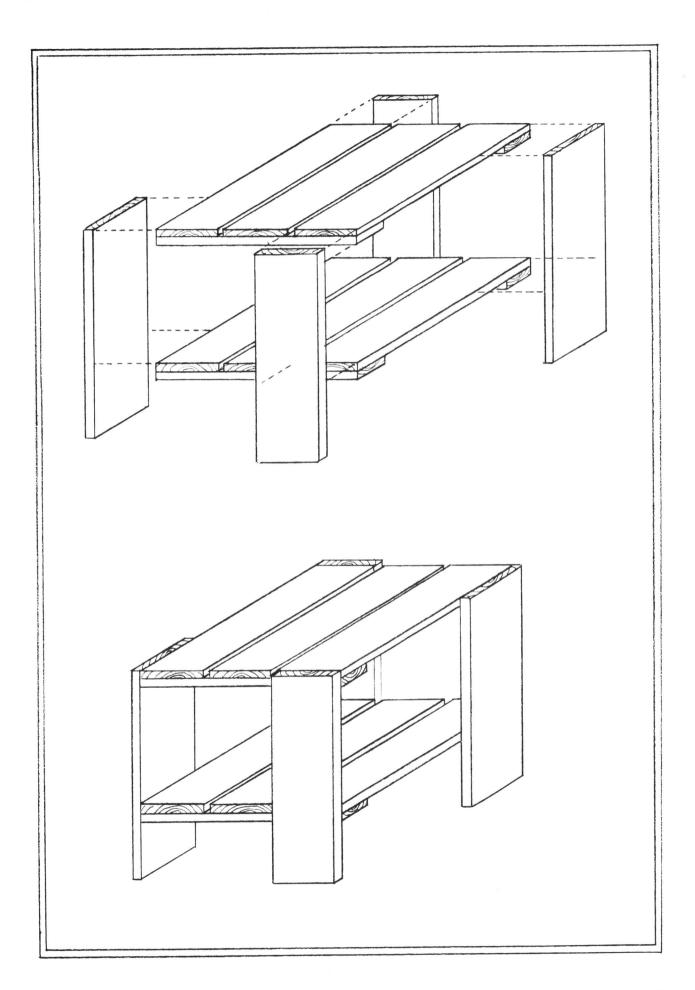

Vocastra 1   Designer: Stamberg

Piece	Section	Quantity	Length	Use
A	1″ × 4″	22	*22¾″	verticals
B		12	*24½″	side slab horizontals
C		6	*25″	back slab horizontals
D	1″ × 2″	14	*26½″	seat slats
E		2	*22¾″	side slabs front trim
F		2	*26″	side slabs top trim
G		1	*25″	back slab top trim

For upholstery see page 34.

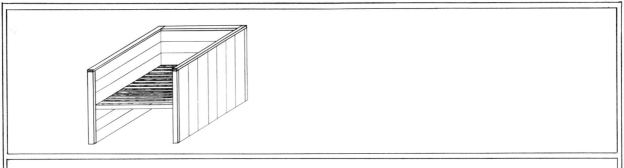

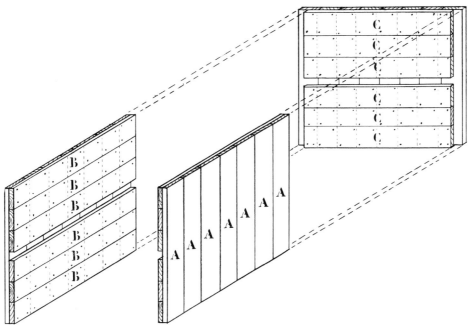

Construct two identical slide slabs using seven A pieces and six B pieces for each. Construct the back slab using eight A pieces and six C pieces. Drive two nails into each B and C piece for each A piece crossed. Remember to glue before nailing.

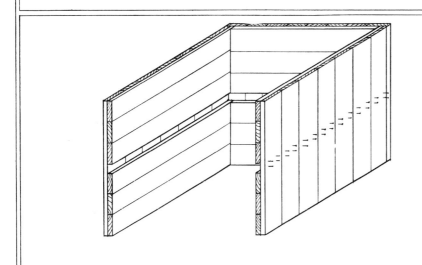

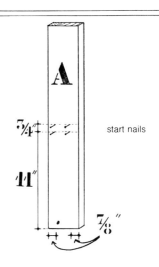

A

3/4"   start nails

11"

7/8"

Before nailing the back slab to the two side slabs, start nails into each A piece on the side slabs as shown to hold the seat slats in position. Then nail the back slab to the side slabs.

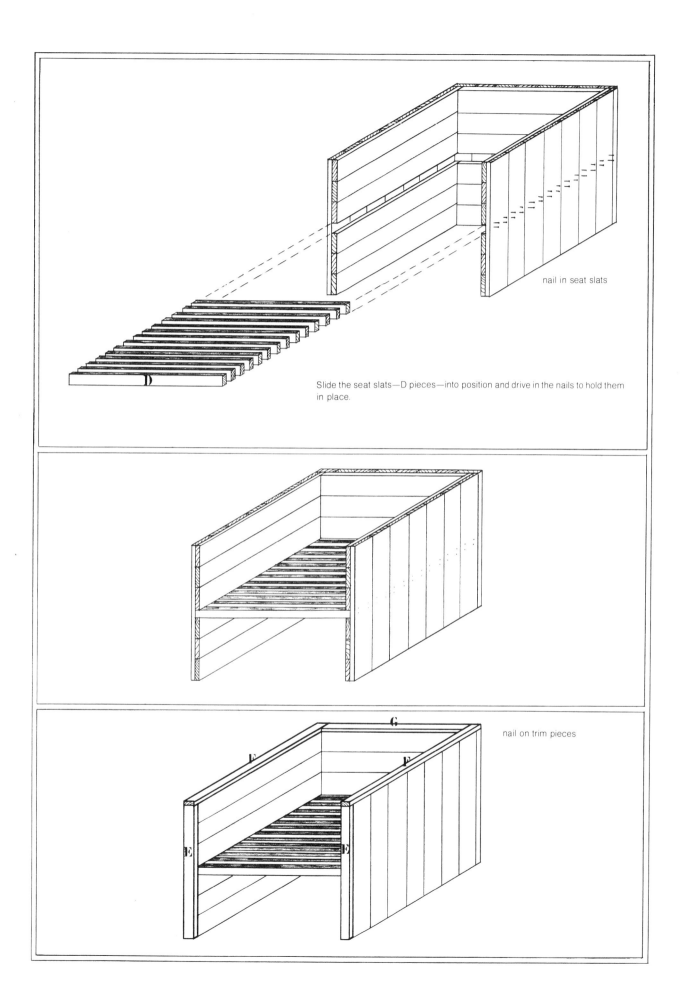

nail in seat slats

Slide the seat slats—D pieces—into position and drive in the nails to hold them in place.

G

F   F

nail on trim pieces

E   E

Vocastra 2   Designer: Stamberg

Piece	Section	Quantity	Length	Use
A	1″ × 4″	29	*22¾″	verticals
B		12	*24½″	side slab horizontals
C		6	*49½″	back slab horizontals
D	1″ × 2″	14	*51″	seat slats
E		2	*22¾″	side slabs front trim
F		2	*26″	side slabs top trim
G		1	*49½″	back slab top trim

For upholstery see page 34.

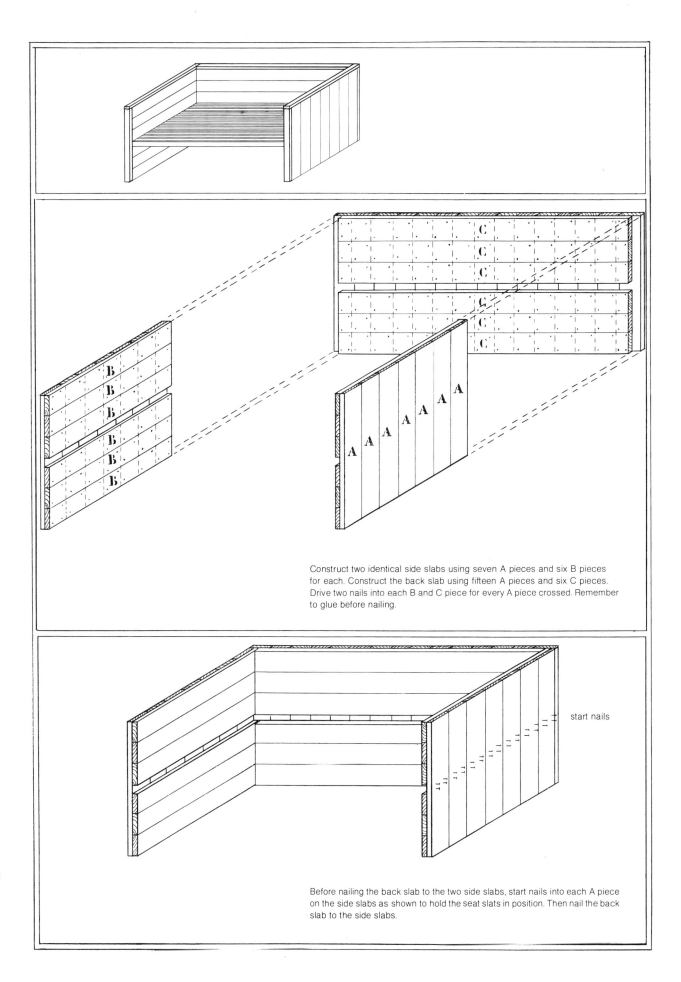

Construct two identical side slabs using seven A pieces and six B pieces for each. Construct the back slab using fifteen A pieces and six C pieces. Drive two nails into each B and C piece for every A piece crossed. Remember to glue before nailing.

start nails

Before nailing the back slab to the two side slabs, start nails into each A piece on the side slabs as shown to hold the seat slats in position. Then nail the back slab to the side slabs.

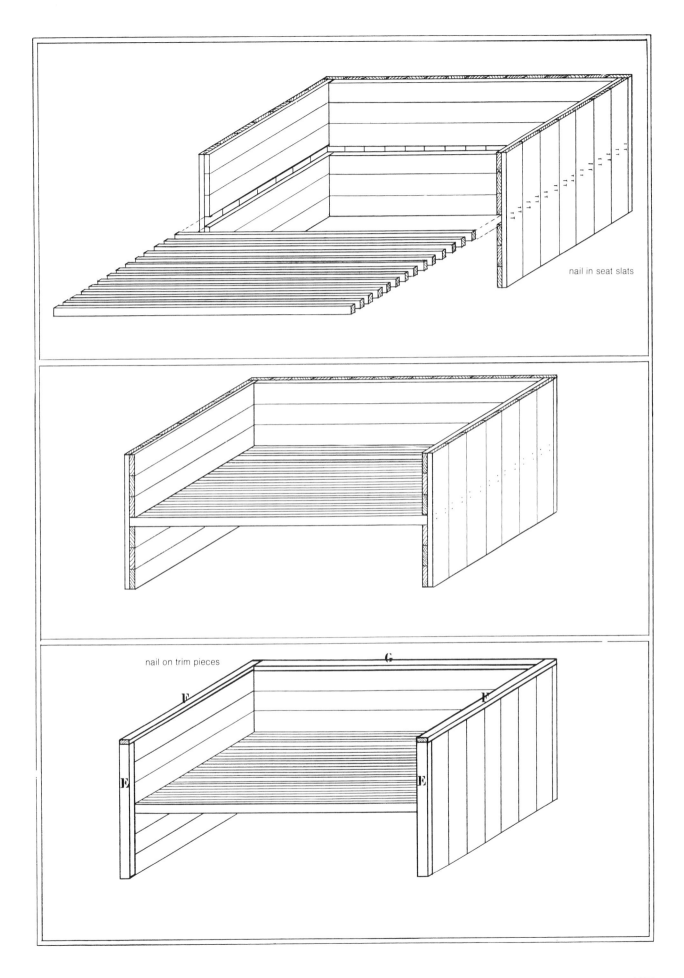

nail in seat slats

nail on trim pieces

G

F   F

E   E

127

DESIGN 29

RioMarin Table   Designer: Carlo Scarpa

Piece	Section	Quantity	Length	Use
A	1″ × 6″	8	27¼″	leg verticals
B		8	54″	top
C		2	*72½″	leg spanners
D	1″ × 4″	8	27¼″	leg verticals
E		9	54″	top
F	1″ × 3″	2	*72½″	top braces

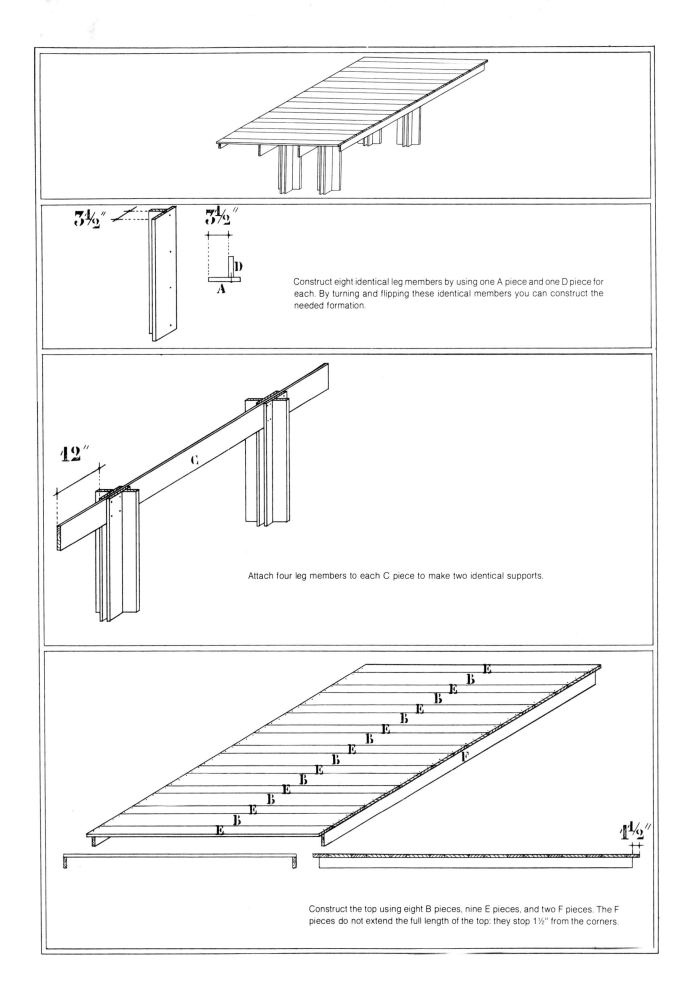

3½″

3½″

Construct eight identical leg members by using one A piece and one D piece for each. By turning and flipping these identical members you can construct the needed formation.

12″

Attach four leg members to each C piece to make two identical supports.

1½″

Construct the top using eight B pieces, nine E pieces, and two F pieces. The F pieces do not extend the full length of the top: they stop 1½″ from the corners.

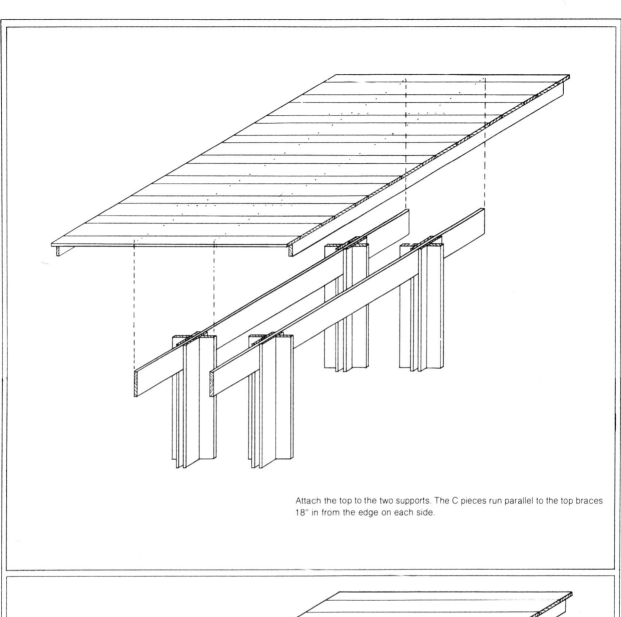

Attach the top to the two supports. The C pieces run parallel to the top braces 18" in from the edge on each side.

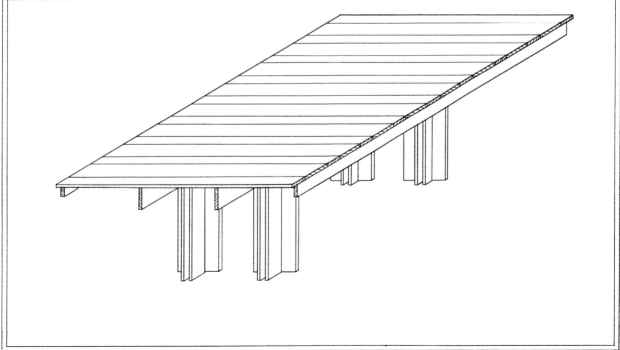

DESIGN 30

Hosonaga Table   Designer: Kazuhide Takahama

Piece	Section	Quantity	Length	Use
A	1″ × 6″	14	28″	top
B		4	27¼″	legs
C		1	54″	spanner
D	1″ × 2″	3	*77″	top spanners
E		4	*11¾″	leg horizontals
F		8	*5½″	L-braces

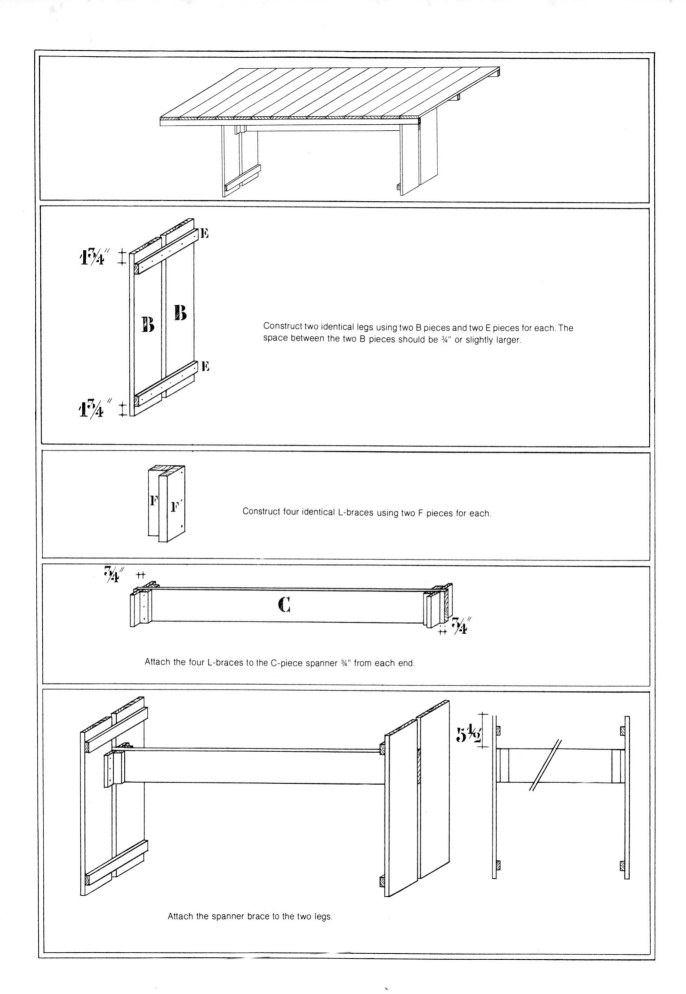

Construct two identical legs using two B pieces and two E pieces for each. The space between the two B pieces should be ¾" or slightly larger.

Construct four identical L-braces using two F pieces for each.

Attach the four L-braces to the C-piece spanner ¾" from each end.

Attach the spanner brace to the two legs.

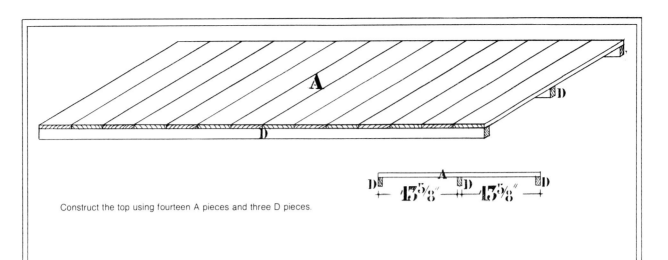

Construct the top using fourteen A pieces and three D pieces.

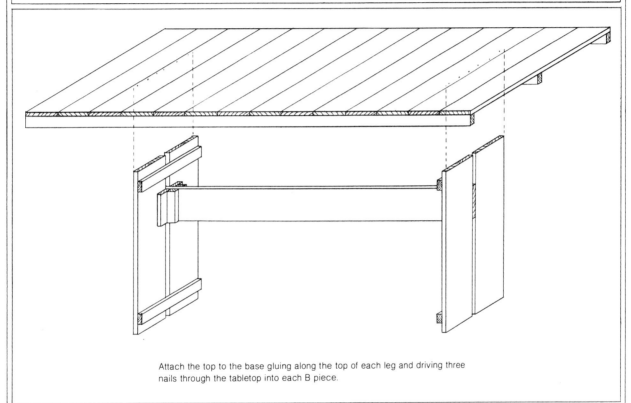

Attach the top to the base gluing along the top of each leg and driving three nails through the tabletop into each B piece.

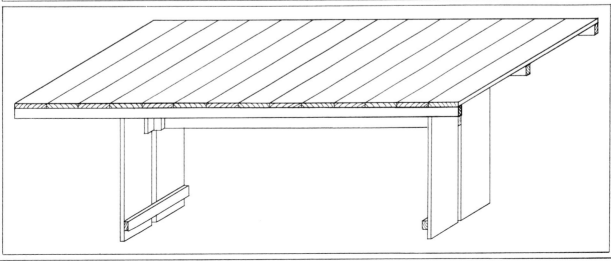

DESIGN 31

DADA   Designer: Kazuhide Takahama

Piece	Section	Quantity	Length	Use
A	1″ × 12″	1	11¼″	small box back
B		1	22½″	long box back
C		6	10½″	small sides
D		2	21¾″	long sides

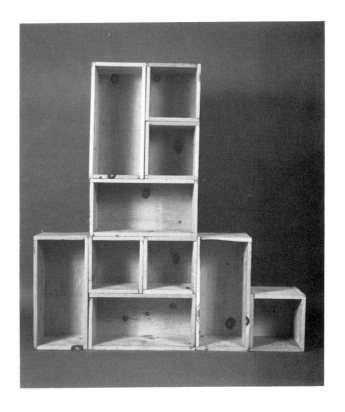

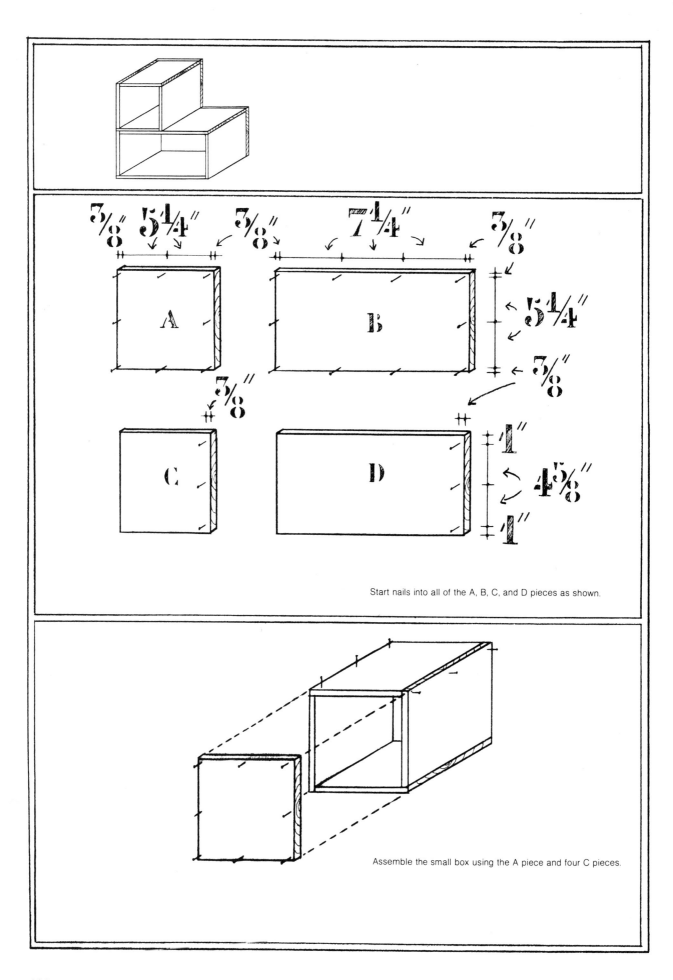

$\frac{3}{8}''$ $5\frac{1}{4}''$ $\frac{3}{8}''$ $7\frac{1}{4}''$ $\frac{3}{8}''$

A   B $5\frac{1}{4}''$ $\frac{3}{8}''$

$\frac{3}{8}''$

C   D $1''$ $4\frac{5}{8}''$ $1''$

Start nails into all of the A, B, C, and D pieces as shown.

Assemble the small box using the A piece and four C pieces.

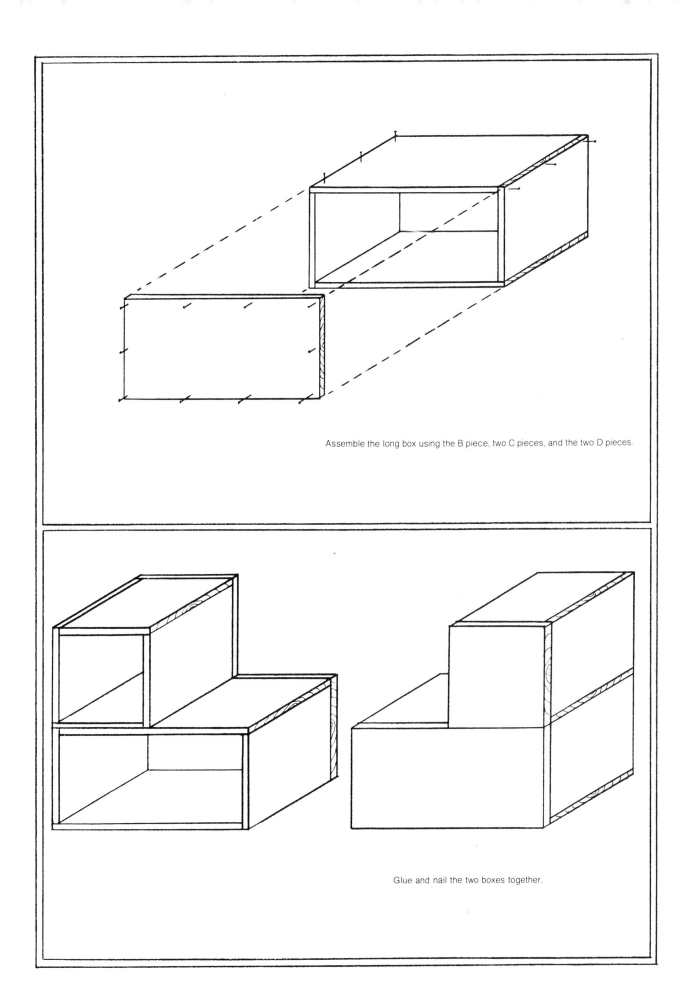

Assemble the long box using the B piece, two C pieces, and the two D pieces.

Glue and nail the two boxes together.

DESIGN 32

Saltz Table   Designer: Ira Saltz

Piece	Section	Quantity	Length	Use
A	1″ × 4″	36	16¾″	sides
B		2	*5″	top
C		2	*12″	top
D		2	*19″	top
E		2	*26″	top
F		1	*33″	top

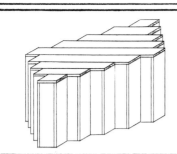

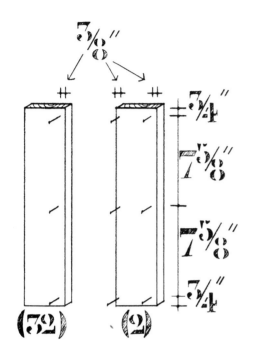

$\frac{3}{8}''$

$\frac{3}{4}''$

$7\frac{5}{8}''$

$7\frac{5}{8}''$

$\frac{3}{4}''$

(52) (2)

Start three nails into each of thirty-two A pieces as shown. Start six nails into each of two A pieces as shown. There are no nails in the remaining two A pieces.

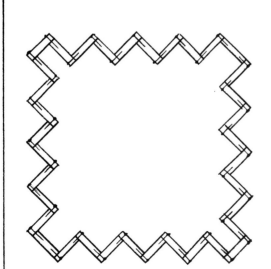

Nail and glue the thirty-six A pieces together in the configuration shown.

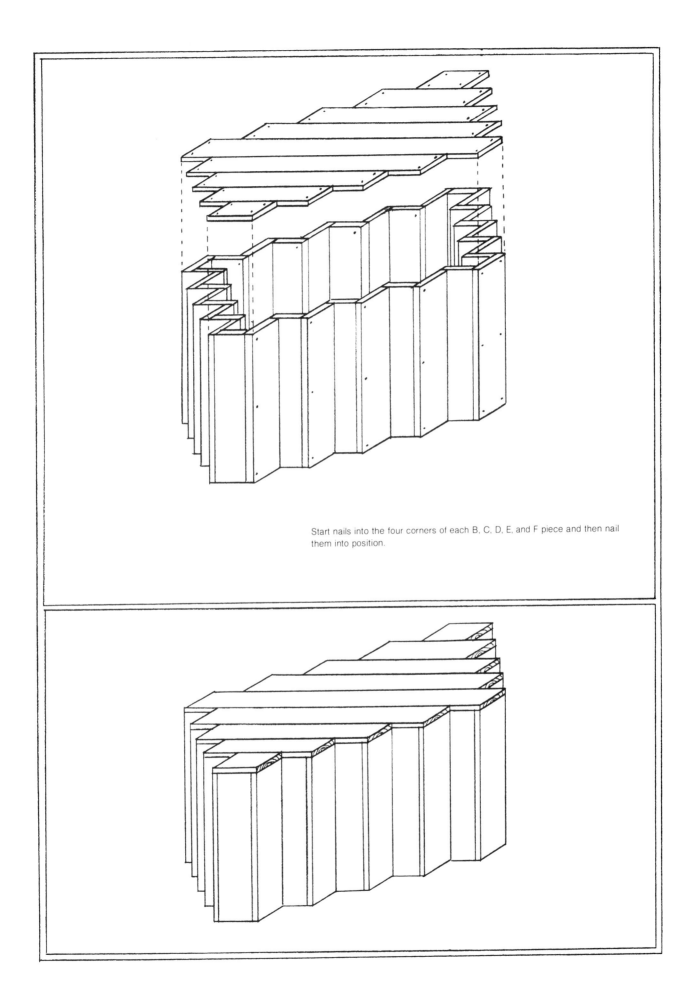

Start nails into the four corners of each B, C, D, E, and F piece and then nail them into position.

DESIGN 33

Marilyn   Designer: Stamberg

Piece	Section	Quantity	Length	Use
A	1″ × 4″	23	31½″	sides & back
B		6	*37″	top
C	1″ × 2″	4	*27¾″	back diagonals
D		4	*21″	side horizontals
E		3	*20½″	top braces
F		2	*35½″	top braces

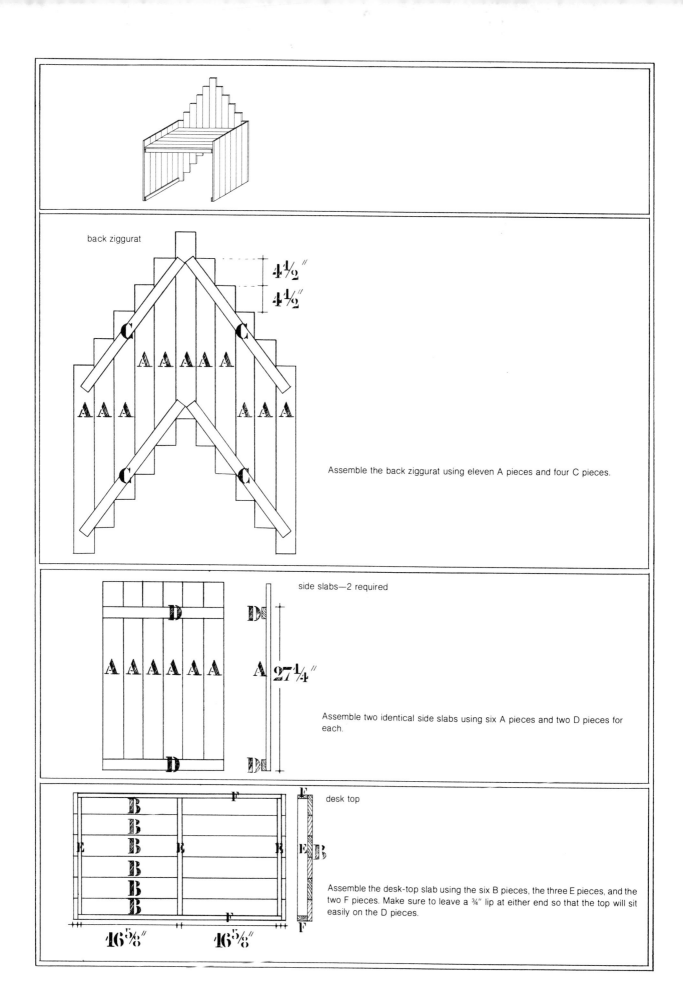

back ziggurat

$4\frac{1}{2}''$

$4\frac{1}{2}''$

Assemble the back ziggurat using eleven A pieces and four C pieces.

side slabs—2 required

$27\frac{1}{4}''$

Assemble two identical side slabs using six A pieces and two D pieces for each.

desk top

Assemble the desk-top slab using the six B pieces, the three E pieces, and the two F pieces. Make sure to leave a ¾" lip at either end so that the top will sit easily on the D pieces.

$16\frac{5}{8}''$ $16\frac{5}{8}''$

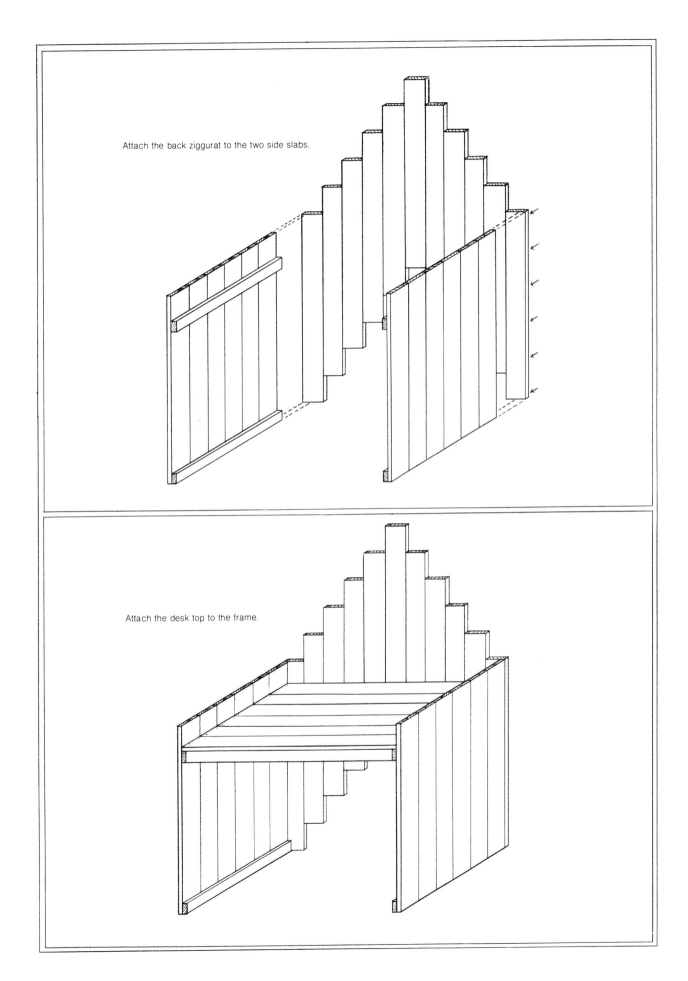

Attach the back ziggurat to the two side slabs.

Attach the desk top to the frame.

DESIGN 34

NLS Desk   Designer: Stamberg

Piece	Section	Quantity	Length	Use
A	1″ × 4″	16	27¼″	leg verticals
B	1″ × 2″	2	*24½″	leg horizontals
C	1″ × 4″	8	60″	top
D	1″ × 2″	2	*28″	top braces
E	1″ × 4″	19	27¼″	pedestal verticals
F		1	*17½″	pedestal front lower fascia
G	1″ × 2″	2	*14½″	pedestal back slab horizontals
H		12	*23¾″	pedestal side slab horizontals
I		6	*16″	pedestal front horizontals
J	1″ × 4″	28	*14″	drawer bottom, front, & back
K		8	*19″	drawer sides
L	1″ × 2″	4	*17½″	drawer front lip

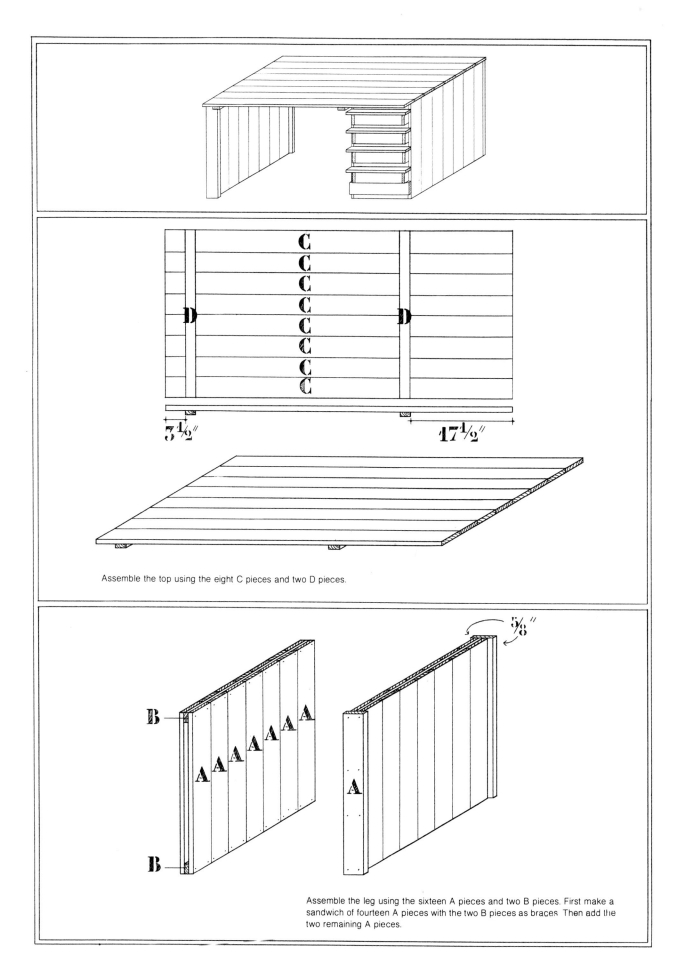

Assemble the top using the eight C pieces and two D pieces.

Assemble the leg using the sixteen A pieces and two B pieces. First make a sandwich of fourteen A pieces with the two B pieces as braces. Then add the two remaining A pieces.

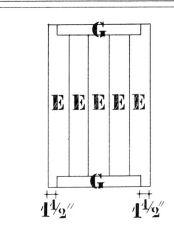

Assemble the rear of the pedestal using five E pieces and the two G pieces.

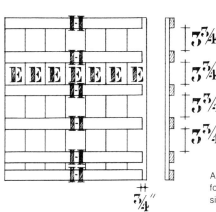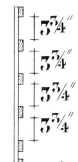

Assemble the two sides for the pedestal using seven E pieces and six H pieces for each. On one side leave the ¾" space on the right as shown. On the other side leave the ¾" space on the left.

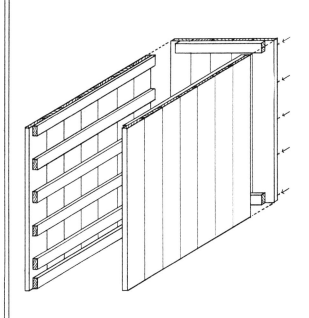

Start nails into the back of the pedestal slab and apply glue.

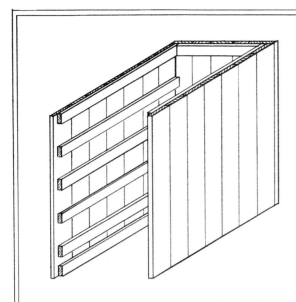

Attach the back slab to the two side slabs.

Glue and nail the six I pieces into position.

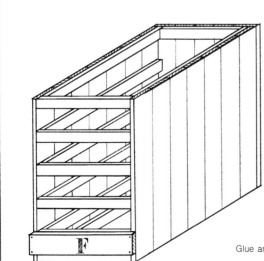

Glue and nail the F piece into position.

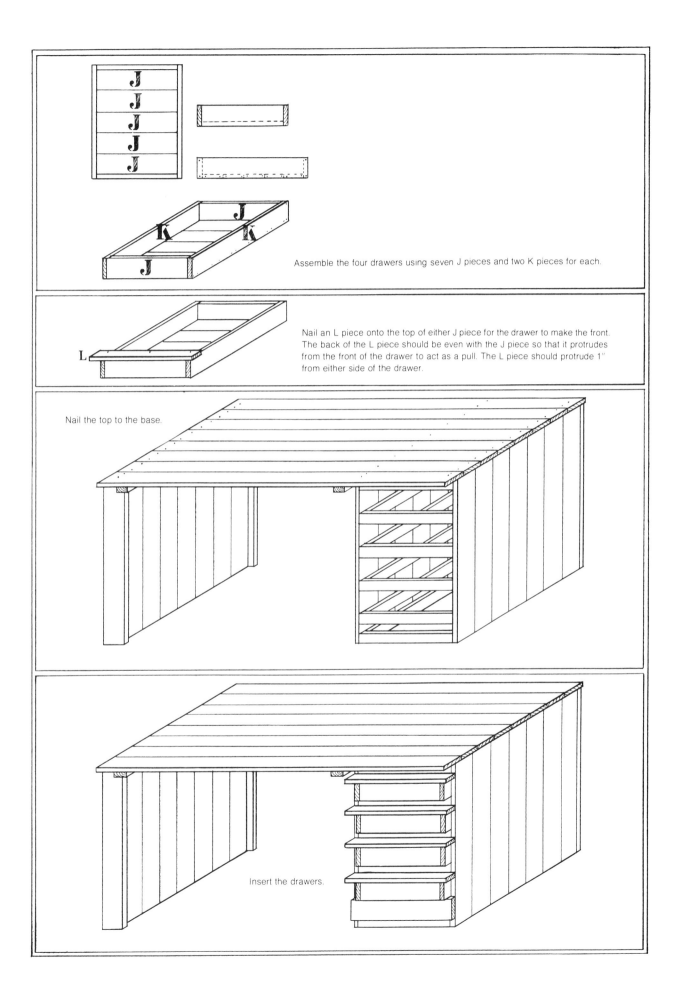

Assemble the four drawers using seven J pieces and two K pieces for each.

Nail an L piece onto the top of either J piece for the drawer to make the front. The back of the L piece should be even with the J piece so that it protrudes from the front of the drawer to act as a pull. The L piece should protrude 1" from either side of the drawer.

Nail the top to the base.

Insert the drawers.